How to Win Intentionally

POWERED FOR SUCCESS

MATTIE NOTTAGE

DR. MATTIE NOTTAGE

ISBN – 978-1-951110-24-6

Published by
Mattie Nottage Ministries, International

www.mattienottage.org

Printed in the United States of America

DEDICATION

This book is dedicated to God, whose unfailing grace has sustained me through every trial, every challenge, and every defining moment that shaped the person I am today. Through His infinite wisdom and faithfulness, He has guided me along the path of true success, teaching me how to draw priceless lessons from every season of life. Whether in moments of triumph or times of adversity, He has shown me that every experience carries purpose and that no encounter is ever wasted in His hands.

I have come to know Him as Jehovah Jireh, the God who faithfully reveals Himself as everything I need, exactly when I need Him. He has been my source, my strength, my provider, and my guide. The principles shared within these pages are rooted in timeless Kingdom truths that have the power to transform lives, cultivate a victorious mindset, and lead individuals toward a life of purpose, fulfillment, and lasting success.

Therefore, this book is also dedicated to every person in pursuit of true success, not simply success as defined by the world, but success that is rooted in purpose, character, faith, and destiny. It is for those who desire more than achievement and long to discover the reason for which they were created. Whether you are standing at the threshold of a new beginning, navigating life's challenges, or pursuing greater levels of growth and fulfillment, it is my prayer that these pages will inspire, empower, and equip you to embrace God's plan for your life and walk confidently in the success He has ordained for you.

ACKNOWLEDGEMENT

First, I acknowledge God the Father, the Son, and Holy Spirit, who is the source and compass of my life. I believe the truths revealed in the pages of this book were divinely inspired by God and will empower believers everywhere to continue pursuing their life's goals strategically and with a winning mindset that honors Him.

To the family, friends, and followers of Mattie Nottage International Ministries and BFOMI Global churches around the world, I appreciate your love and support. Thank you for your prayers and faithfulness. *Powered For Success* was written to help you elevate to the winner's circle God's way!

PLANNING FOR SUCCESS

TABLE OF CONTENTS

Chapter 1
Journey To Success..8
Processed Through Failure..9
The Irony Before The Triumph..10
Failure: One Of My Greatest Teachers..12
Failure Before Victory..13
Defeat Vs Failure..14
Pathway To Success..16
Failure Is Not Final..18

Chapter 2
Mindcology..20
Battle For The Mind..21
Enemies Of Successful Minds..23
Mental Attacks..26
The Spirit Of Fear..27
Breaking Demonic Cycles..28
The Purge Is Necessary To Win..29
Winning Through A Consecrated Mind..29
Steps For Prayer And Consecration..30
Discovering And Rediscovering Your True Self..31

Chapter 3
Wisdom And Divine Timing..34
The Wisdom Principle..35
Winning With Wisdom..36
Winning At A National Level..37
Window Of Opportunity..38
Navigating Life's Challenges..40
Your Divine Season Of Manifestation..41
From Barren To Blessed..42
It's Your Time To Give Birth..43
Broken And Not Barren..44
Preparing For Change..46
The Divine Realm Of Possibilities..47
The Power To Embrace Change..48

Chapter 4
Winning Is A Lifestyle..........50
The Lifestyle Of Winning..........51
Winning Intentionally..........52
Good Success Vs Bad Success..........53
The 10 P's Of Success..........55
How To Have True Success In Your New Season..........68
Practical Steps For True Success..........69
Godliness With Contentment..........73

Chapter 5
The Winner's Mindset..........74
How You See What You See..........75
Winners Make It Happen..........76
Gates: Divine Opportunities..........77
Persistency In Success..........79
Secrets Of Successful People..........80
My Idea Of Success..........82
People The World Call Successful..........83

Chapter 6
Powered From the Secret Place..........86
The Power Of Radical Prayer..........87
Prophetic Prayer Codes For Success..........89
Succeeding Through Serving..........93
Succeeding Through Sacrificial Giving..........94
Succeeding Through Forgiveness..........95
Purpose Of Fasting..........96
Succeeding By Fasting..........98
The Importance Of Studying The Word..........98
Succeeding By Studying The Word..........100
Succeeding By Meditation And Rest..........100

Chapter 7
Spiritual Intelligence..........104
Force Of Faith..........105
Dreams, Visions & Destiny..........106
Spirit-Led Intelligence..........109
Spiritual Magnetism..........112

Wisdom Of A Sound Relationship....................................113
The Law Of Attraction.. 116
Attraction In Godly Relationships....................................116
Spiritual Mutualism.. 118
The Law Of Attraction In Kingdom Business....................119

Chapter 8
Destined To Win... 122
Understanding Gifts, Talents and Abilities...................... 123
Core Personality Traits.. 124
The Power Of Networking.. 127
Goal Setting.. 129
Living Life At The Mastery Level...................................134
The Mark Of Master Builders..................................... 137
Anointing And Unction To Win.................................... 139
You Will Win...141

INDEX.. 146
Author Information...147
Ministry Contact Information..................................... 150

JOURNEY TO SUCCESS

"But seek ye first the kingdom of God, and his righteousness; and all these things shall be added unto you." Matthew 6:33 KJV

CHAPTER ONE

PROCESSED THROUGH FAILURE

Success has a way of revealing itself long before it is ever understood. Long before titles, influence, or measurable outcomes, it shows up quietly, as potential, as a gift, or as a knowing placed deep within the soul that there is more within you than your current circumstances can contain.

In my early years, I was always aware that I carried something special: an unusual gift, a drive, and a sense of calling that refused to be ignored. Yet this awareness did not lead to an easy path. In fact, the very seasons that should have validated my promise became chapters marked by disappointment, detours, and repeated setbacks. What felt like momentum on the inside often collided with what looked like failure on the outside.

For a long time, I believed that failure proved I had misread my life. I mistook delay for denial and resistance for disqualification. Like many, I was taught to see success as a straight line that always moves forward, predictable and steadily upward. Yet real success does not always emerge from clearly defined linear paths. It is forged in pressure, refined in obscurity, and often introduced through seasons that make no sense at all. The scriptures expressly reveal that Jesus learned obedience through the things He suffered (Hebrews 5:8).

What I did not understand then but have come to know is that failure is not the opposite of success but often its training ground. The very moments that felt like breakdowns were actually opportunities to build a framework, strengthen character, reshape my thinking, and align my life with a deeper, more sustainable definition of success.

This book was not born out of achievement but out of a life-changing process. It was shaped by the tension between promise and reality: between what I believed was possible and what I repeatedly experienced. Powered for Success is not about arriving quickly; it is about being properly prepared. It is about learning to think, recover, rebuild, and advance when life does not immediately reward you.

If you have ever felt gifted yet stuck, called yet delayed, or capable yet misunderstood, this book is for you. If you have ever questioned whether your failures disqualify you from success, this book will challenge that belief, because true success is neither accidental nor reserved for the flawless. It is built by those willing to learn, endure, and rise with wisdom. This is not a story of perfection. It is a story of power, developed, refined, and ultimately unleashed. Welcome to *Powered for Success*.

THE IRONY BEFORE THE TRIUMPH

I truly believe every authentic success story contains an irony rarely discussed and almost never celebrated. Before the thrill of victory, there is often the quiet humiliation of defeat. Before applause, there is isolation. Before confidence, there is uncertainty. Before a breakthrough, there is almost always a loss.

What makes this irony so powerful is that defeat does not announce itself as preparation. It feels final, personal, and like proof that you miscalculated your ability, misunderstood your timing, or overestimated your capacity. Yet again and again, life reveals a paradox: the very moments that seem to dismantle us are often the ones that position us. I learned this not through theory but through lived experience.

Like many purpose-driven, faith-filled, and risk-taking people, my husband and I believed that stepping out in boldness would naturally lead to success. We did what responsible, hardworking people are taught to do. We invested, built, planned, and launched. We started our own car lot business with vision, optimism, and the confidence that diligence alone would carry us forward.

We truly believed we were in a blessed season, but instead, we entered a season of unraveling. What began with excitement slowly gave way to pressure. Decisions that once felt strategic grew heavy. Our momentum stalled, then one loss led to another. The business failed, and with it, everything we thought we had secured. We did not just lose a company; we lost our first home, our cars, and our possessions. In a short period of time, the life we had built collapsed beneath us, and there was nothing we could do about it.

There is an unexplainable pain you sometimes feel when failure seems to cost you everything. This pain can weigh more heavily than losing money, because the failures that cause it can cost you your reputation, your identity, and even your peace of mind. These failures may greatly threaten the success you are about to achieve, but as confusing and uncertain as these times were, we soon came to understand that all things truly work together for good once we learned to consult God during our seasons of failure. (Romans 8:28)

FAILURE: ONE OF MY GREATEST TEACHERS

In our case, we experienced one of the greatest disappointments in our entrepreneurial pursuits: we did not fail because we were reckless or passive; we failed while trying to do everything right. That irony was difficult to comprehend, let alone explain to many people.

Defeat does not always come to the unfaithful or the unprepared. Sometimes it comes to those who are brave enough to step forward before they fully understand the arenas they enter. Sometimes loss is not punishment; it is experience: experience that highlights gaps and inconsistencies in thinking, exposes gross assumptions, and delivers painful lessons that help mature one's way of thinking and operating.

Looking back, I now understand that we were not losing our future; we were being stripped of false perceptions and unprofitable delusions. We were learning that success without structure is fragile; that vision without wisdom is vulnerable; and that ambition without alignment can collapse under its own weight.

In the end, we determined that the experience taught us to rebuild on something stronger than mere enthusiasm and the simple hope that all things would somehow work out. We soon found, however, that if we were going to achieve true success in our endeavors, our decisions had to be well thought out, our actions deliberate, and our attention focused.

This is the space where I began learning the strategies you will discover flipping through the pages of this book. One of these key strategies is that success does not truly begin at the peak, but in the valley. It does not arise in the height of victory, but from obscure situations. In other words, real success does not emerge from avoiding defeat but from learning to interpret it, intercept it, and rise above it. The thrill of victory is never as powerful as when you understand the cost it took to achieve it.

FAILURE BEFORE VICTORY

After years and years of what felt like repeated failure, I discovered a space where potential and performance did not always align. It is in this space that most people encounter bouts of failure; not once, but time and time again. No one wants to fail at something they are committed to watching grow. However, as I continued pursuing my passion and what God was calling me to do, I realized that no matter how hard I tried, I did not get everything right.

As I worked to keep myself encouraged after each unsuccessful encounter, I soon found myself dissecting those experiences. The more I dissected them, the more I made mental notes to watch for certain pitfalls and missteps. I implemented stronger precautions to avoid repeating those mistakes, and I found that the more I confronted my failures, the more I learned what not to do.

Then I realized that there were little lessons, even in the failures, that taught me just as much, and even more, than when everything worked out right. When you are in the moment, failure can be confusing because it forces you to face the gap between what you expected and what your life reflects.

Failure does not always arrive dramatically. Sometimes it shows up quietly, in endeavors that almost work, ideas that seem promising yet never fully take shape, and seasons when effort does not yield results. These are not moments of collapse;

they are moments of reckoning and resolve. It is crucial to resolve moments of failure quickly because, if left unresolved, they will weigh on the soul over time. I lived with unresolved failures for years. I was gifted, driven, and deeply aware that I carried more on the inside than my outcomes revealed.

Despite ability and intention, I failed again and again. I do not believe that I was unsuccessful because I lacked vision. On the contrary, I had visions of great things, but I soon understood that vision alone is not enough. Having a vision is just the first step toward achieving something great. You must have a carefully laid-out plan that will bring your vision to pass. Once your vision is carefully laid out, you must put effort into it. However, effort without understanding eventually exhausts itself. All of it must work together to make your plan the reality you dreamed of.

DEFEAT VS FAILURE

Defeat feels heavier than failure because it implies finality. Failure suggests you can try again. Defeat, on the other hand, convinces you that something has been taken from you. It challenges not only your strategy but also your identity. It is here, between failure and defeat, that the greatest irony of success lies.

My husband and I lost all our possessions. What we thought were secure possessions began disappearing little by little. In a short period of time, the life we had worked so hard to build unraveled completely.

This was not just a financial loss; it was emotionally and mentally painful and, without a doubt, spiritually disorienting. The most painful reality is that we were not reckless. We were not lazy. We were not irresponsible. We failed even as we believed and trusted in God, wholeheartedly doing everything right.

Over the years, my husband and I encountered many fundamental factors that led to periods of failure. Sometimes, you may experience failure because of the cost of entering environments you have not yet mastered. Other times, you may encounter failure because you did not engage in a practice long enough, or, conversely, you were engaged in a practice too long and should have shifted your efforts before incurring the loss. Whatever the catalyst for the failure, experience is always the tuition for acquiring wisdom.

What I understand now is this: failure exposed gaps; defeat stripped away illusions; and both were necessary to prepare us for a level of success that could endure any circumstance. Therefore, before the thrill of victory comes clarity, before abundance comes alignment, and before sustainable success is ever achieved, something within us must be rebuilt.

The difficult lessons of failure we experienced taught me not to glorify loss but to redeem its value. I have come to learn that the greatest success stories do not begin with triumph; they begin with the courage to fail, the humility to learn, and the strength to rise again with understanding.

PLANNING FOR SUCCESS

PATHWAY TO SUCCESS

More often than not, success is not readily seen or even perceived. In some instances, it is hidden within the tapestry of potential, hinting at great possibilities that require the right formulas, the right force, and the right resources to reach full maturity. Long before results appear, a pathway and a process are necessary to help you succeed. There is an unshakable "knowing" that there is more inside you than your current life can explain. In Romans 12:3, the word of God reveals that a measure of faith has been given to every man:

"For I say, through the grace given unto me, to every man that is among you, not to think of himself more highly than he ought to think; but to think soberly, according as God hath dealt to every man the measure of faith."
Romans 12:3 KJV

From an early age, I carried that awareness. I knew I was gifted. I knew I was driven. I sensed purpose before I had the language for it. Yet, the early chapters of my life were not marked by consistent wins; they were marked by failure. Not a single moment of collapse, but repeated experiences in which effort exceeded outcome, promise outpaced performance, and things that should have worked simply did not. Failure became familiar long before victory ever did.

What made it difficult was not the failure itself but the contradiction it created. How could gifting coexist with struggle? How could vision live alongside disappointment? How could hard work and dedication lead to failure? I worked hard. I showed up. I believed it. Yet time and again, I faced outcomes that did not reflect my capacity. Failure has a way of making you feel humiliated. It can make you doubt your ability or worth.

It is not always obvious, but it can sometimes appear as missed opportunities, stalled responses, or seasons when progress feels unattainable.

You may be bombarded with more questions than answers, including questions no one can adequately answer. These include questions such as: Am I capable? Did I misunderstand my calling? Am I doing what God has gifted me to do? Is success meant for someone else? Struggling with the reality of not getting it right all the time, or with prolonged disappointments, may create a mindset steeped in the thought of failure that arises when you meet defeat.

GROWING PAINS: MILLIONS OF DOLLARS…GONE!

Yes, you read it right. That is exactly what happened! Before seasons of success, my husband and I lost millions of dollars, even after aggressively executing our carefully defined business model. Earlier in life, we eagerly pursued the opportunity to start our own business. As we stepped onto the path of entrepreneurship, and approached this new venture expecting to succeed. Neither my husband nor I was afraid of hard work. Like everyone else, driven by their vision, we believed that courage, faith in God, and due diligence would automatically lead to success.

As mentioned, we started our own car lot business with expectations and confidence, believing we were finally stepping into the season our efforts had prepared us for. Instead of immediate success, we encountered major roadblocks, some big and some small; however, they all worked together to create a wealth of do's and don'ts for our master executive business plan.

The failures began as small miscalculations, slow seasons, and decisions that did not deliver what we expected. At first, these seemingly minor missteps were manageable, nothing major, just learning curves as we continued to build our business. Unfortunately, we soon learned that when you do not fully understand the mistakes and shortfalls you have made, you risk compounding failure and eventually suffering defeat. Without a relationship with God and genuine trust in His plan for our lives, I firmly believe my husband and I would have succumbed to defeat.

FAILURE IS NOT FINAL

After much prayer and careful introspection, my husband and I regrouped and learned a lesson so valuable that no amount of money could buy: resilience during times of difficulty or defeat determines how much you gain from unexpected failures.

Romans 8:28 reminds us that all things work together for the good of those who love God and are called according to His perfect plan. Similarly, we can say that failure is not destruction but merely an indicator that something needs to be revisited or restructured.

Consider the story of Thomas Edison, who famously refused to view his thousands of unsuccessful attempts as failures. Instead, he saw them as discoveries, simply thousands of ways that did not work. With each attempt, he gained valuable knowledge and moved one step closer to success.

The same principle applies to our lives. The setbacks, disappointments, and obstacles you encounter are not wasted experiences. They are lessons that build wisdom, strengthen character, and prepare you for what lies ahead. Every challenge you overcome and every mistake you learn from brings you closer to your purpose and ultimate success. Therefore, rather than allowing failure to discourage you, you should allow it to educate, refine, and propel you forward, because what may appear to be a setback today could very well be the steppingstone that leads you to your greatest breakthrough tomorrow.

This book begins here, not at the peak of success, but in times of growth disguised as failure. It is not in the glory of applause, but in the pressure of preparation. It is about understanding how setbacks shape thinking, how loss builds character, and how wisdom is forged long before results are visible. The thrill of victory is powerful, but it is meaningful only when you endure the adversity required to prepare for it. That preparation almost always begins with defining your true purpose and final intent for your ambitions and working toward that end goal.

MINDCOLOGY

"Casting down imaginations, and every high thing that exalteth itself against the knowledge of God, and bringing into captivity every thought to the obedience of Christ;" 2 Corinthians 10:5 KJV

CHAPTER TWO

BATTLE FOR THE MIND

You will never achieve true success if your mind is constantly embattled. Many people are controlled by evil powers and demonic entities because they have not yet gained an understanding of who they are in God. This is due to the fact that the enemy begins to infiltrate the mind with erroneous thoughts, hindering the mind from functioning as the mind of Christ. These people begin to live a life of dysfunction to the extent that they are unable to succeed, as their mind becomes their biggest enemy.

"For we wrestle not against flesh and blood, but against principalities, against powers, against the rulers of the darkness of this world, against spiritual wickedness in high places." Ephesians 6:12 KJV

"For though we walk in the flesh, we do not war after the flesh" 2 Corinthians 10:3 KJV

To live a successful life, you must raise an altar of consecration. Though many people give their lives over to Christ and are delivered from demonic entities, the dilemma is that the minds of many of these people are never renewed. The mind is one area of a Christian's life that does not simply renew itself; it must be deliberately sought after and renewed. The mind must undergo renewal and deliverance.

Many people go through life feeling unaccomplished and attribute it to superficial factors. However, in many instances, this sense of ill accomplishment stems from negative effects on the mind, thoughts, and overall stability.

Housed within the arena of the soul are the mind, will, intellect, and emotions of man. Today, we spend more time grooming and developing the physical body, giving no thought to the soul. However, we must come to understand that while the soul comprises the very identity of a person, the body is merely the vehicle for the spirit and the soul.

For many, the gateway of the soul has been wounded because they have given themselves over to others more than to God. In doing so, they become trapped in perpetual cycles of brokenness and injury.

The gateway of the soul is the entryway to your entire being. When God created man, He breathed into us, and we became a living soul. Therefore, if our souls are not nurtured spiritually and properly aligned with the framework of Christ, we can experience hurt, pain, and suffering. With this in mind, you must ensure that the gateway of the soul is a gateway of fire. Likewise, you must ensure that those closely connected to you, including your loved ones, have passed through the gate of fire.

Anyone in your life who hasn't undergone the refining process symbolized by the gate of fire can be used by Satan to speak discouraging words to you in your weakest moments, deterring you from your purpose. To enter the arena of the soul, you must first pass through the gate of fire.

ENEMIES OF SUCCESSFUL MINDS

The enemy often attacks people through bloodline curses, witchcraft operations, and the altars of the wicked. Yet within each of these categories lie countless ranks of demonic forces that seek to influence and control the soul and mind. Many of these spiritual entities serve as gatekeepers, standing at the entrance to the mind and soul, attempting to regulate thoughts, emotions, decisions, and spiritual perception.

One of the greatest weapons the enemy uses to attack the mind is self-will. Self-will places personal desires, opinions, and ambitions above the will of God, causes people to resist correction and instruction, and instead, pursue their own agenda. What begins as a desire for control or bad habits eventually becomes a stronghold that hinders spiritual growth and prevents people from walking fully in God's purpose.

The enemy also works through negative thought patterns, planting seeds of fear, doubt, insecurity, rejection, hopelessness, and unbelief. If these thoughts are not confronted with the Word of God, they can take root and develop into strongholds. Over time, a person begins to think, speak, and act according to these lies rather than according to God's truth.

A stronghold is a fortified mindset that is resistant to change. It includes deeply rooted beliefs, arguments, and thought patterns that exalt themselves against the knowledge of God. Their purpose is to keep the believer from recognizing their authority, identity, and victory in Christ.

If you are going to experience victory in any area of life, you must first win the battle in the mental arena. The war for your destiny often begins in your mind. Therefore, you must guard your thoughts, strengthen your spirit through prayer, renew your mind by the Word of God, and refuse to surrender your soul to the enemy.

In many instances, people who are attacked in their minds are unaware of the attack, and it takes a spiritual person to open their eyes to this mental dilemma. Demonic strongholds may enter a person's life through self-annihilation, self-mutilation, and personal destruction. Some people develop personal habits that, if not checked, can take over their thoughts and entire being. I have seen many people who were destined to succeed, taken out by demonic strongholds that terrorized their minds, causing defeat.

Here are some of the ways the enemy attacks successful minds:

- Trauma
- Pharmakeia (Drugs)
- Substance Abuse (Alcoholism)
- Witchcraft (Demonic Arrows)
- The Bloodline
- Self-Humiliation
- Pride
- Abuse
- Unforgiveness
- Willful Sin
- False Accusations

How Demons Attack The Mind: Blocking Success

Demons are evil spirits, and they do not ever want you to succeed in life. This is our spiritual warfare as Christians. Therefore, they will afflict you in many ways such as:

- Memory Loss
- Anxiety
- Insanity
- Bipolar Disorder
- Insomnia
- Loneliness
- Isolation
- Chronic Depression
- Schizophrenia
- Anti-Intelligence Spirits
- Dumb Spirits
- Arrested Development
- Low Self Esteem
- Lethargy
- Laziness
- Procrastination
- Suicidal Thoughts
- Doubt & Unbelief
- Mental Illness in Children: (Autism, Dyslexia, Mental Retardation, Suicidal Thoughts, etc.)

MENTAL ATTACKS

"Be sober, be vigilant; because your adversary the devil, as a roaring lion, walketh about, seeking whom he may devour:" 1 Peter 5:8 KJV

Signs That the Mind Is Under Attack

- Gross Depression
- Bipolar Disorder
- Extreme Isolation
- Wall-Out Spirit
- Self-Condemnation
- Forgetfulness
- Unpredictable Actions
- Racing Thoughts
- Superstitious Mind
- Anxiety Attacks
- Nervous Breakdowns
- Fears
- Phobias
- Schizophrenia
- Multiple Personalities
- Psychotic Behaviors
- Zombie-Like Behaviors

Gateways To Mental Afflictions

- **Rejection From the Womb**
- **Childhood Hurt**
- **Broken Relationships**: (Family, Marriage, etc.)
- **Trauma**
- **Tragedies**
- **Self-Inflictions such as:**

- *Occult Practices*: The use of evil powers and spirits, including spiritism and other influences to control others' lives. (e.g., Freemasons, Witchcraft Practices, Eastern Stars, Fraternities, Sororities, Secret Orders, etc.)
- *Drugs and Alcohol* which leads to mental affects such as hallucinations.

- *Cutting habits* that open the door to demonic spirits
- *Certain Tattoos*
- *Certain Piercings*

- **Witchcraft Attacks**
- **Ancestral/ Bloodline Curses**
- **Abuse**

Various Forms of Abuse:

- *Emotional*	- *Religious*
- *Verbal*	- *Relational*
- *Mental*	- *Sexual*
- *Financial*	- *Physical*

It is important to understand that while some of these gateways may come through circumstances beyond a person's control, others are opened through personal choices. In many cases, individuals unknowingly give access through the doors they open, whether through willful sin, associations, or other evil practices. Simply put, some people may be in part, responsible for the doors they open and the influence those doors have on their mental and spiritual well-being.

THE SPIRIT OF FEAR

Fear can be considered one of the greatest enemies to your success. It has brought giants to their knees and brought the fastest people to a screeching halt. It has kept geniuses from inventing life-changing creations and kept musicians from producing number-one hits. Fear can hijack your progress and undermine your confidence just when you need it most.

PLANNING FOR SUCCESS

As you step into this new season, you must recognize fear as an adversary and confront it head-on. By doing so, you can overcome it and unlock the door to your success. You must embrace the power of faith and trust in God's guidance to find favor and victory in your endeavors.

Fear, along with other negative forces such as pride and doubt, can keep you from achieving your best. It can keep you from writing your best book or sharing your story, which could change the world. To find favor and success in the coming year, you must overcome fear.

Fear often works hand in hand with pride. When fear doesn't paralyze you, pride steps in and tells you that you are too powerful, too big, or too intelligent for the task at hand. These thoughts are meant to deter you from your purpose.

Another adversary to success is doubt, along with its close companion, unbelief. Together, they can poison a person's path to progress and fulfillment. These forces foster a toxic mindset that leads many to abandon their goals rather than persevere until they achieve them. I have personally faced these adversaries, but I can confidently say I have overcome them all. It took believing in God, trusting His plan, and finding the strength within myself to defeat these evil spirits. Like the little train that could, I kept telling myself, "I think I can, I think I can," until I did. I often quoted scripture and refused to dwell on or dwell in negative thoughts.

BREAKING DEMONIC CYCLES

Many people become introverted as a result of the trauma and pain they have experienced. They isolate themselves and allow little to no one into their personal space because they feel compelled to protect themselves. The danger with introverts lies in the fact that they often overthink. One may never truly comprehend what is going on in the mind of an introvert until they are made angry or "rubbed the wrong way." These are called demonic triggers and take place because an incident occurs that reminds a person of the hurt and pain they have experienced in the past. Thus, causing a relapse.

THE PURGE IS NECESSARY TO WIN

- You will never enter your divine purpose in Christ.
- You will never succeed or gain victory in life.
- You will never enter the place of absolute freedom.
- You will continue living in demonic cycles.
- You will begin carrying the spirit of guilt.
- You won't be able to distinguish between those who are out to hurt you and those who genuinely care.

WINNING THROUGH A CONSECRATED MIND

"A consecrated lifestyle will position you to have a consecrated mind!" Dr. Mattie Nottage

Although a personal battle may be raging in your mind, we have been given the power to win the warfare in the mind through various spiritual tools and strategies. One such tool is the raising of an altar of consecration. When facing battles in the arena of the mind, an altar of consecration must be raised against the mind's deviancy, pessimism, and negativity.

PLANNING FOR SUCCESS

Consecration goes beyond mere salvation as God calls the church to a higher level of relationship, dedication, and devotion. Further, consecration implies a lifestyle of holiness unto God and is a realm of spiritual existence that requires you to absolutely turn away from evil habits.

Many people sometimes feel like their lives are stagnant and that they're being hindered, whether it's related to promotions, success, relationships, or things of the like. Although this sense of stagnation can be attributed to spirits such as delay, hindrance, and blockage, to get to the root of this problem, you must be true to yourself and ask: What do I need to be purged of?

STEPS FOR PRAYER AND CONSECRATION

- A desire must first be present for true prayer.
- Once a desire is present, prayer must become a habit. It is said that it takes 21 days to form or break a habit.
- Prayer must then become a practice. When prayer is practiced, it becomes more effective. Practicing prayer should not be considered a mere ritual; if it is, let it be a positive and holy one.
- Next, prayer must become a part of your daily routine.
- After these several steps, prayer becomes a lifestyle. This involves being committed, dedicated, and completely sold out to prayer (having a resolute mind).

DISCOVERING AND REDISCOVERING YOUR TRUE SELF

In essence, discovering who you truly are and understanding the purpose for which you were created is a life-changing realization. You begin to recognize that your presence on earth is not accidental but intentional. You were created with value, purpose, and significance. You are an asset, not a liability; a contributor, not a burden. As you embrace your God-given identity, you come to understand that your gifts, talents, and experiences were designed to meet specific needs and positively impact others' lives. When a need arises, God can position you as part of the solution, using your life to bring value, help, and transformation wherever He sends you.

Think of something as simple as a screw. A screw was invented because someone recognized the need to hold things together. Imagine if the screw thought it was insignificant, saying to itself, "I'm just a small, twisted piece of metal with a big head. I have no purpose." Without screws, many things would fall apart. Although a screw and a nail may look similar, they serve different purposes. A nail cannot replace a screw because it lacks the grooves that allow the screw to twist and lock in place. It takes a specific tool, a screwdriver, to remove a screw.

God is saying today that whether you see yourself as a screw, a nail, or even the hole the screw fits into, you have a divine purpose in life. Never forget or overlook your purpose, because God promises favor and good success to those who observe and do all that He has commanded. (Joshua 1:8) God's promise is clear: you will experience good success, and your way will be made prosperous if you keep His words in your mouth and meditate on them day and night. Begin each day with great anticipation in your heart. God knew you before you were formed in your mother's womb. He knows everything about you, from the number of hairs on your head to what makes you happy or sad. He has equipped you with everything you need to succeed. So, start commanding your day, and you will witness phenomenal changes unfolding around you.

WISDOM AND DIVINE TIMING

"To every thing there is a season, and a time to every purpose under the heaven." Ecclesiastes 3:1 KJV

CHAPTER THREE

THE WISDOM PRINCIPLE

"Wisdom is the principal thing; therefore get wisdom: and with all thy getting get understanding"
Proverbs 4:7 KJV

Someone can either give you a fish or teach you how to fish. While being handed a "fish" may seem beneficial in the short term, providing temporary support and provision, learning skills from those carrying the anointing of greatness far surpasses this. Teaching someone to fish goes beyond providing immediate relief; it promotes independence and equips individuals with the valuable skills needed to grow, develop, and ultimately succeed. When people are equipped with the knowledge and skills to fend for themselves, they gain control over their situation and are positioned to achieve total and absolute victory. In this old but true adage, learning to fish represents acquiring lifelong lessons that can be applied in specific areas of life to meet needs, foster change, and win the victory.

This sense of empowerment leads to independence and prepares individuals for spiritual maturity. Contrary to popular belief, spiritual maturity is not defined by a specific age but by a stage of gathering wisdom. This wisdom hides in the corridors of those who possess humility and those who desire knowledge and understanding.

Wisdom will come alongside you, prompting and enabling you to ascend into realms and dimensions within the spiritual realm. Those possessing gifts without wisdom often find themselves at the brink of breakthrough but can never fully enter the doors of opportunity, as there is no wisdom to sustain the blessings they have attained. Thus, in addition to gifts, talents, and abilities, you must seek God for wisdom to further foster these endowments and maintain them after entering the doors of breakthrough.

Many individuals desire to win and succeed in life. However, winning must first become a passion and a habit, and the only way to win is through the wisdom of God, which is not sensual. This concept can be seen in the lives of many individuals who were least likely to succeed yet nonetheless achieved success through the wisdom of God.

For instance, Joseph, the beloved son of his father Jacob, possessed the powerful gift of dreaming, which left his brothers in a state of jealousy, envy, and resentment. Because of their jealousy, they conspired and acted against Joseph, hiding his body in a pit and later selling him into slavery. What separates Joseph from the average Christian, however, is his steadfastness and confidence in God amid immense adversity. Despite the many injustices faced by Joseph, he remains faithful to God, steadfast in his integrity, and confident in God's supernatural abilities.

WINNING WITH WISDOM

"Wisdom is the principal thing; therefore get wisdom: And with all thy getting get understanding. Exalt her, and she shall promote thee: She shall bring thee to honour, when thou dost embrace her. She shall give to thine head an ornament of grace: A crown of glory shall she deliver to thee." Proverbs 4:7-9 KJV

Wisdom is the ability to discern inner qualities and relationships. It is knowing what is right from wrong. It is the ability to apply knowledge and experience to make sound decisions and judgments.

Using wisdom on the road to success is very important, as the lack of wisdom is one of the primary causes of failure. While talent and resources are often attributed to success, without wisdom, these factors can never lead to it. Operating without wisdom can be extremely detrimental to a person's pursuit of victory, as it often leads to poor decisions, irrational or impulsive behavior, poor connections and relationships, missed opportunities, and ultimately, failure.

When you possess the wisdom of God, success is inevitable because it equips you with the discernment to see the true motives and intentions of those around you. Godly wisdom also gives you divine strategies to succeed in situations that appear impossible and positions you for victory in every area of your life.

WISDOM AT A NATIONAL LEVEL

El Salvador was once marked by crime and violence, but now serves as a prime example of how the wisdom of God can shift entire regions and lead to success. When journalists asked the President of El Salvador about his strategy for turning one of the most dangerous and violent nations in the world into one of peace, his answer shook many. Surprisingly, his response did not revolve around policymaking or a change in laws but was quite simple yet bold: "The wisdom of God." He did not refer to the wisdom of man or other human strategies, and this shows that true success can only be attained when we take the time to tap into the wisdom of God.

This required him to go against worldly advice from others, which may even have led them to view him as conventionally unfit to be a leader. However, the wisdom of God guided every decision he made, enabled him to stand firm amid chaos and criticism, and brought him ultimate success.

WINDOW OF OPPORTUNITY

"I returned, and saw under the sun, that the race is not to the swift, nor the battle to the strong, neither yet bread to the wise, nor yet riches to men of understanding, nor yet favour to men of skill; but time and chance happeneth to them all." Ecclesiastes 9:11 KJV

Many demonic spirits are sent from the gates of hell to prevent a person from entering the doors of opportunity. The first demon waiting at the gate of an opportunity is:

- **CRISIS.** A crisis can present itself as an unexpected problem or a dilemma you did not anticipate. If you are not careful, at the onset of a crisis, you will fail to seize your God-given opportunities.

- After a crisis comes the demon of **INTIMIDATION**. Intimidation is defined as the act of making timid or fearful, and occurs when an individual believes they are incapable of becoming or achieving something specific.

- When intimidation has set in, the demon of **FEAR** will seek to manifest. What crisis and intimidation failed to do, fear will accomplish. Fear will cripple and immobilize many people, so that at their greatest gateway, they fail to enter.

These gates serve as obstacles, hindering the progress of many. They seek to manipulate, intimidate, and control individuals' destinies. At the gates of opportunity, territorial demons will always be present. They appear in every shape and size, inform you of what you "cannot" accomplish, and ultimately attempt to turn you away from your gates of opportunity.

In like manner, poverty is a wicked spirit that brings evil into the lives of those who bear it. Because of this dilemma, individuals living in poverty often find themselves doing things they would never normally do, or even lowering their standards.

You may be full of gifts, power, and anointing; however, if poverty is upon you, others often lose respect for you. Though you may possess scores of gifts, talents, and abilities, poverty essentially renders you a vanishing vapor, with no one remembering your life.

For instance, the Bible mentions a wise yet poor man who was used by God to deliver the city from the hands of an evil king who had taken the opportunity to lay siege to and overtake it. Through his God-given wisdom, the wise man devised and executed a plan to save and deliver the city. Nonetheless, because of his poor economic and financial position, his noble deed was remembered by no one. Simply put, due to the wise man's poverty, he appeared irrelevant to the city, though he performed such a mighty act, and he was remembered by no man.

"14There was a little city, and few men within it; and there came a great king against it, and besieged it, and built great bulwarks against it: 15 Now there was found in it a poor wise man, and he by his wisdom delivered the city; yet no man remembered that

same poor man. [16] Then said I, Wisdom is better than strength: nevertheless the poor man's wisdom is despised, and his words are not heard." Ecclesiastes 9:14-16 KJV

Though the Bible states that we will always have the poor with us, we should not aspire to live in poverty, as it also states that God desires us to prosper and be in health, even as our soul prospers.

"For ye have the poor always with you; but me ye have not always." Matthew 26:11 KJV

"Beloved, I wish above all things that thou mayest prosper and be in health, even as thy soul prospereth."
3 John 1:2 KJV

NAVIGATING LIFE'S CHALLENGES

With the anointing, believers are better equipped to face and overcome life's challenges. The Holy Spirit provides:

- **Strength:** In times of difficulty, the Holy Spirit strengthens believers, giving us the resilience to persevere and remain faithful.

- **Guidance:** When faced with tough decisions, the anointing offers clear direction, helping believers to discern the best path forward according to God's will.

- **Peace:** Amidst chaos and uncertainty, the Holy Spirit brings peace that surpasses all understanding. This peace guard believers' hearts and minds, allowing us to remain calm and trust in God's sovereignty.

YOUR DIVINE SEASON OF MANIFESTATION

BREAKING THE CURSE OF STAGNATION

Stagnation is a physical or spiritual condition in which a person is unable to move forward or accomplish anything substantial in life. Whenever someone is stagnant in the natural, that person is unable to bring projects, tasks or assignments to completion., although they possess everything they need to do so. Whenever someone is plagued with a spirit of stagnation, that person is unable to manifest the dreams, visions and ideas given to him by God.

In the book of *Genesis 1:27–28,* God released a four-fold assignment over the life of Mankind and made him to be *fruitful, multiply, subdue* and *replenish* the earth. Stagnation was never a part of God's plan for your life. He created you with an ability to create, produce and reproduce.

When you are unable to produce, in various seasons in your life, then you may be challenged with a spirit of barrenness. There are a number of other factors that can also attribute to someone's barren condition. In the natural, if a person harbors deep-seated issues of unforgiveness, resentment, bitterness or hatred in their soul, sometimes the result could be the development of ulcers, cysts, tumors, fibroids and other medical maladies.

These and other issues such as generational curses, old age and some disorders can create barrenness, birth defects, miscarriages and other devastating issues in a person's life. In some instances, it appears as if, God allows some people to be barren in order to show forth His glory. He does not get glory out of the "barrenness." However, He gets glory when He steps in and turns the situation around.

We can see this in the lives of people like Sarah, Abraham's wife, who, in the fullness of time, brought forth Isaac. We can also see this in the life of Rachel, Jacob's favored wife. Although she was the apple of her husband's eye, she was also barren. However, in the fullness of time, God opened her womb, and she brought forth Joseph. He was one day elevated to a seat of governing authority in the land of Egypt and later used this position to save his family and the nations of that time from a destructive famine.

FROM BARREN TO BLESSED

Hannah, was the wife of Elkanah and the mother of the Prophet Samuel. She had spent the majority of her life in a barren condition, unable to bear children. On the other hand, Penninah, who was also Elkanah's wife, was very fruitful. As a result of her barrenness, Penninah scorned and ridiculed Hannah for her inability to produce a child. Because of her embittered situation, Hannah set herself to seek God for divine intervention, asking Him to grace her with a son.

It was not only her fervent request that got God's attention, but it was her vow to rededicate this child to Him that caused the hand of God to move in her favor. Hannah gave birth to one of the most profound prophets of that day in the person of Samuel. From the day his mother took him to the temple and left him in the hands of God to the day of his death, he remained completely sold out and dedicated to the office of the prophet.

I believe that more than Hannah wanted a son, it was God who wanted a prophet to be born. I believe that if Hannah had not been barren that she would not have sought the Lord as she did. It was her condition of barrenness that caused her to press into the presence of God.

You may be waiting for God to move on your behalf in many situations. However, in some instances, God may be waiting for you to come in agreement with Him concerning the matter. Once your prayers begin to align with the Spirit of God He will begin to move on your behalf and your prayers would have prevailed.

"IT'S YOUR TIME TO GIVE BIRTH!"

1 To everything there is a season, and a time to every purpose under the heaven: 2 A time to be born, and a time to die; a time to plant, and a time to pluck up that which is planted; 3 A time to kill, and a time to heal; a time to break down, and a time to build up; 4 A time to weep, and a time to laugh; a time to mourn, and a time to dance; Ecclesiastes 3:1- 4 KJV

The number nine represents birthing. In this season of your life, God Himself will initiate a spiritual rebirth in you. Whether you are man, woman, boy or girl, you should know that you have a spiritual womb. However, it is important to know that the enemy will seek to attack your "spiritual womb" in order to cause you to lose your dream, vision or idea. There are four (4) types of attacks that would seek to come against the womb of a mother.

These attacks also have spiritual implications, which include, but are not limited to:

- **Barrenness**
- **Spiritual Miscarriage**
- **Spiritual Abortion**
- **Infant Mortality Death**

The enemy often seeks to use the spirit of death in conjunction with the spirits of barrenness, miscarriage and abortion, to prevent you from giving birth. He wants your spiritual womb to be non-productive, inactive and dormant.

However, God desires that you come into a season where your womb can be shifted....*but the shifting is predicated on faith, your willingness, and your desire.*

BROKEN AND NOT BARREN

Have you ever been to a place in your life where you felt as though you were somehow broken? You are not quite sure but you wrestle with the feeling that you should be further ahead in life or more productive but you feel stuck. You go through your entire life without ever accomplishing any of your goals or aspirations.

The "sledge hammer" of life's circumstances have left you so hurt and discouraged that you have lost the courage to ever want to give birth to anything ever again. You will know when something has attached itself to you to hinder, block and stifle your progress. The spirit of death works along with a spirit of barrenness. To be *"barren"* means to be non-producing, unable to bear children.

In the book of Mark 11:21, Jesus cursed the fig tree because it did not have any fruit on it. The spirit of barrenness was a sign that the tree was supposed to be producing in that time and season but it was not. As long as your spiritual womb (mind) is infected by poisons and toxins such as offense and hurt, bitterness and others, conception will never take place. Some of the spirits and issues which help to perpetuate barrenness are: *malice, jealousy, strife, heaviness, depression, sadness*

A few years ago, I was conducting a revival service. At the end of preaching and teaching the Word, I felt a strong leading of the Holy Spirit to minister deliverance to two groups of persons. These persons were married but without children and the other group was those who wanted to be in business or their business was struggling to produce.

Out of the first group three women came to the altar. They were all weeping and I could see the desperation in their eyes because they each wanted to have a baby. I anointed and prayed for them. Then the Holy Spirit revealed to me that each one of them was holding on to past hurts and had failed to forgive the person who had hurt them.

Two of the women immediately began weeping even more intensely, repeated the prayer of deliverance and willfully forgave their offenders. The other lady just stood there and appeared to be very angry. She said that she was not ready to forgive the person who hurt her because she wanted the person to be punished and to suffer. I asked her when was the last time she saw or spoke to the person, she said over fifteen years ago.

Needless to say, the two women who were eager to forgive their predators have both seen supernatural wonders in their lives. In fact, one of them became pregnant with twins a year later. The power and keys of forgiveness cause you to walk in total freedom and releases you from the daunting dungeons of life's prison of death.

PREPARING FOR CHANGE

During the many years of counseling and advising individuals, I have come to realize that one of the main factors in life that remains the same is "change." Many times people make career changes, changes in living arrangements, relational changes, lifestyle changes and the like. It would seem in life that nothing remains the same, except God Himself.

By definition, change is a variation in routine; a difference in doing something; or the act of making or becoming different, revolutionizing, transforming or adjusting. In the New Testament, the Greek word often associated with transformation is **metamorphoō** (μεταμορφόω), from which we derive the English word **metamorphosis**, meaning transformation, change, or transmutation

Change is necessary for your progress!

[2] And be not conformed to this world: but be ye transformed by the renewing of your mind, that ye may prove what is that good, and acceptable, and perfect, will of God. Romans 12:2 KJV

There are 3 basic dimensions of change which include:

The Power to Change

This is an ability given to each individual, whether by internal design or external means in order to affect change in his/her life. This simply means that change is available and accessible to everyone

The Power of Change

is a power that comes as a result of a change - in attitude, position, status, mindset, etc. this means that once an individual embraces change, this decision empowers him/her above his/her circumstances; they are no longer, weak, timid or afraid

The Power <u>for</u> Change

This is a power that affords an individual to become an agent or catalyst for change; because he/she decided to embrace the opportunity for change around them, they now have the power or the ability to affect change in their personal life, the life of others, in their community and/or culture

THE DIVINE REALM OF POSSIBILITIES

It is a proven fact that unless a person truly wants change, they will never do anything about their present situation or circumstance. In other words, most people remain stuck in their same dilemma year after year because they have not made a resolute decision for radical change. Some people become complacent and tend to disqualify themselves by settling with the notion that "this is it" and that nothing is going to change for them. Further, others have been in their situation so long that they tend to adopt the mindset that things will not change; after all that is the way it has always been.

If you find yourself battling any level of defeat, today I would like to cancel all such erroneous beliefs and dispel every diabolical lie that the enemy has spoken to you. I overthrow and superimpose a life-changing prophetic declaration to you that God is willing and well able to turn everything around that you are going through right now. I activate your spiritual mind to the "Divine Realm of Possibilities" where Jesus said that all things are possible to them who believe.

THE POWER TO EMBRACE CHANGE

It is amazing to see how many people *"need to change"* or *"need a change"* but refuse to do what is necessary to embrace it. It would seem as if some people make themselves comfortable and become resolved in their minds that the place where they are, even though it is unaccomplished, wearisome and depressing, is where they need to be. They live a life of frustration, vexation and hardship - not willing to leave their place of familiarity to find change.

They choose rather to remain tied to the enemy of their past by reliving painful historic experiences rather than setting sail for undiscovered worlds beyond the scope of their claustrophobic imagination. They allow their minds to remain tied to an old mindset and a mundane culture like an old boat which is tied up in a harbor, never setting sail to new horizons.

"As long as your boat is tied to a dock, it will never leave the harbor." Dr. Mattie Nottage

I firmly believe that Change is necessary for your progress. If you are ever going to progress or move forward in life, you must embrace Change. In other words, you must have an open mind to welcome the changes that will take place in and around you, recognizing that nothing will remain the same.

Every second brings something new. Sixty seconds equals a minute and after sixty minutes we get what is called a new hour. The protocol shifts and changes every moment while we are alive. Every day you change. You change your hair, your clothes and sometimes even your friends. Remember, life is built on the premise of change, and it continues to change as long as you are alive.

WINNING IS A LIFESTYLE

"For whatsoever is born of God overcometh the world: and this is the victory that overcometh the world, even our faith." 1 John 5:4 KJV

CHAPTER FOUR

THE LIFESTYLE OF WINNING

The term "winning" is used across many areas of society, including sports and gaming, and is often discussed in a secular context. However, the concept of winning is not limited to basketball games or the annual Super Bowl. In fact, winning is a lifestyle many people aspire to but often fall short of.

> **Success Translations**
> **Hebrew**- *Hatzlacha*
> **Greek**- *Epitychia/Nike*
> **Latin**- *Successus*

Thus, the question of "What does it truly mean to win?" arises. Though this may seem like a simple question, the average person has not yet fully grasped the concept of winning. In literal terms, winning means achieving victory or success in a given task. Winning can be defined as achieving victory or overcoming a perpetual struggle or entity, according to 1 John 5:4.

"For whatsoever is born of God overcometh the world: and this is the victory that overcometh the world, even our faith."
1 John 5:4 KJV

Like many chapters of the Bible, this verse emphasizes the idea of believers as winners. While many people find their sense of victory in superficial factors such as wealth or material gain, every believer has already been deemed a winner because of one simple yet powerful factor: a firm belief in the death, burial, and resurrection of Christ. Because of our belief in Christ and through God's gift of salvation, we, in essence, died with Christ, have been raised with Him, and share in His victory over the kingdom of darkness.

God's desire is not for you to experience success for a single day, but to cultivate a lifestyle of winning and a lifetime of success. Over the years, I have discovered that one of the greatest hindrances to success is seeking validation and explaining your "Why" to people who have never accomplished what God has called you to do. Many dreams have died because their owners listened to the opinions of individuals who lacked vision, understanding, or experience. Had I followed the counsel of ignorant people, I would not be where I am today.

Truly successful people often cannot fully explain why they do what they do. They are driven by revelation, conviction, and purpose. To the natural mind, their actions may seem foolish. Yet history consistently shows that what seems foolish in one season often becomes the breakthrough everyone celebrates.

WINNING INTENTIONALLY

You can choose to win by luck or chance, or to win intentionally. The choice is yours but remember that those who win by chance or luck often forget how they won, and their victory is often short-lived. When the moment comes to compete again, they struggle, not because they lack the necessary skills or abilities, but because they lack an understanding of the strategies that led to their victory. They are not sure how they won the first time.

People who win intentionally are different. They do not leave success to chance or luck; instead, they plan, practice, and continually build on their strengths. They study carefully, adjust their strategies, and strengthen their approach to ensure that success is not only intentional but inevitable.

Winning intentionally causes you to develop a formula and a strategy for success. Once that formula is implemented, a pattern emerges and becomes solidified. In fact, because this formula has been proven reliable in attaining success, it can be carried from one generation to another. This is because winners keep their brand, and their recipe for success becomes consistent.

GOOD SUCCESS VS. BAD SUCCESS

Good success is something everyone can identify with. For the most part, when you hear the word success, it carries a positive connotation. If success automatically carries a positive connotation, the question arises: why does the Bible mention good success? (Joshua 1:8) This implies the possibility that someone can achieve bad success, since the qualifier 'good' suggests its opposite exists.

"This book of the law shall not depart out of thy mouth; but thou shalt meditate therein day and night, that thou mayest observe to do according to all that is written therein: for then thou shalt make thy way prosperous, and then thou shalt have good success." Joshua 1:8 KJV

Because the writer makes a clear distinction by using the word "good" when describing success, we can imply that not all success is good, and therefore, one can infer that there is also bad success.

PLANNING FOR SUCCESS

Success, though often associated with something positive and beneficial, can be extremely detrimental to a person's overall growth, development, and maturity if it is not rendered and imparted by Christ. "Surely, success can in no way be negative," some may believe. However, if your success does not originate from Christ and is not rooted and established in Godly principles, it will not only be entirely short-lived but will also do more harm than good.

In today's day and age, it is commonly said that money, the hallmark many equate with success, cannot purchase or guarantee a life of happiness. However, those looking from the outside may consider this a fallacious cliche until they are placed in this predicament. Many individuals, though they may appear to have the perfect life, with wealth, riches, and fortune, are often addicted to drugs and alcohol, are depressed, or are overtaken by the urge to take their own lives. Why bring deliberate affliction upon your life if success truly only brings happiness and prosperity? This is what I call bad success.

Bad success refers to a lifestyle of seemingly good fortune that is not God-given, rooted, or established, and may often be disguised as a life of peace, joy, and prosperity. This success often involves an extravagant lifestyle, not a Godly one. It distracts you, masks your true identity in Christ, and pulls you away from your God-ordained assignment and, ultimately, from serving God.

When pursuing success, it is essential to remember that true success can only be achieved through prayer. It is also important to note that if your success does not come from God, it is the enemy's plan disguised as prosperity, which ultimately leads to defeat and perpetual failure.

THE 10 P'S OF SUCCESS

Over the years, I have discovered many key principles and strategies for achieving success. These are what I call the 10 Ps of Success, and they are as follows:

- **Pray**
- **Potential**
- **Purpose**
- **Passion**
- **Plan**
- **Prepare**
- **Pursue**
- **Practice**
- **Plant a seed**
- **Produce**

PRAY

"But without faith it is impossible to please him: for he that cometh to God must believe that he is, and that he is a rewarder of them that diligently seek him." Hebrews 11:6 KJV

Believing that God exists and that He will reward you if you diligently seek Him is the primary requirement for receiving answers, direction, and instructions from God. Though our relationship with God should not be based solely on our desires, it is of the utmost importance to pray to God about them. In fact, the Bible clearly exhorts us to "cast all our cares on Christ, for He cares" (1 Peter 5:7). This is not the only biblical case in which we are instructed to present our desires to God, as Philippians 4:6 states:

"Be careful for nothing; but in everything by prayer and supplication with thanksgiving let your requests be made known unto God." Philippians 4:6 KJV

It is important to note that true success is found only in God and can be achieved only through a lifestyle of consistent, persistent, and sincere prayer unto God. Whenever a person in pursuit of success prays for the establishment of their goals, visions, and ideas, they are far more likely to succeed, because they place their plans before the throne of God in faith for ultimate victory.

Trials and tribulations are bound to occur in life, especially when pursuing success; therefore, through the integration and implementation of prayer, God makes a way even in the midst of life's dead ends, turns our captivity into prosperity, and grants us true success.

When we place our goals, dreams, and aspirations before God in prayer, we acknowledge our need for Him in our pursuit of success. We also recognize that without God's guidance and wisdom, we can never achieve anything of great value. This acknowledgment fosters humility and invites divine intervention as we, unworthy beings in need of a savior, seek God's help. When we pray, we are more likely to succeed by submitting our goals, plans, and desires at the feet of Jesus rather than attempting to accomplish them by our own strength.

When you truly pray to achieve a specific goal or succeed at a specific task, God gives you the plan and instructions to accomplish it, whether through visions of the night, creative wisdom, strong impressions, or other similitudes. These open the door to success and serve as a roadmap that guides the believer. This can be seen in the life of David, who was least expected to succeed yet achieved great success through the corridors of prayer.

POTENTIAL

To achieve any level of success, you must first tap into your potential, that is, your untapped abilities. Potential is the hidden reservoir of ability, talent, capacity, and possibility that exists within a person before it is fully manifested. It is the unseen greatness waiting to be discovered, developed, and deployed. Potential is not who you are today but who you can become tomorrow. In fact, every invention, every business, every leader, and every ministry began as potential.

Simply put, potential is the bridge between your present reality and your future possibility. It is God's investment in you before the world ever recognizes your value, and it is the seed of success. Just as every forest is hidden within a seed, every success story is hidden within potential. Before David became king, he had the potential to lead. Before Joseph governed Egypt, he had the potential to manage nations. Before Esther saved her people, she had the potential to influence a kingdom. Success is often the visible manifestation of previously hidden potential. Many people admire the fruit but forget the years of cultivation that brought it to fruition.

The Difference Between Potential and Performance

One of the greatest misconceptions is that potential and success are the same thing. They are entirely different. Potential is what you can do, while success is what you actually do. Potential is possibility, while performance is execution. Potential opens the door, while performance walks through it. The difference between potential and success is evident in the fact that a person can possess extraordinary potential yet accomplish very little if they never develop discipline, character, and consistency.

The Tragedy of Untapped Potential

The greatest loss in life is not money; it is unrealized potential. Many people die carrying:

- *Unwritten books*
- *Unlaunched businesses*
- *Undiscovered inventions*
- *Unfulfilled callings*
- *Unused gifts*
- *Unspoken ideas*
- *Unfinished assignments*

They possessed the potential but never fully developed it, unlike those who refuse to let their potential remain dormant and, in doing so, change the world.

The Enemies of Potential

There are many enemies that can pose a hinderance to your potential. Some of this may include:

- **Fear**: Keeps potential imprisoned and convinces people to stay where they are; it whispers: "You're not ready." "You'll fail." "What will people think?"

- **Procrastination:** Every day of delay is a day when potential remains undeveloped. Potential requires action; dreams become reality only when action is applied consistently.

- **Lack of Vision**: People cannot pursue what they cannot see. Without vision, potential often remains hidden beneath the surface. Vision reveals potential. "Where there is no vision, the people perish." Proverbs 29:18 KJV

- **Negative Environments:** Potential thrives in healthy environments and struggles in toxic ones. Some people never discover their potential because they remain in environments that suppress growth.

- **Lack of Discipline:** Talent may open doors, but discipline keeps them open. Potential without discipline rarely leads to lasting success.

PURPOSE

Purpose is the reason someone or something was created, designed, assigned, or intended to exist. In human life, purpose is the divine assignment, mission, or intended function for which a person is born.

Characteristics of Purpose

Purpose has distinct characteristics that people often overlook. Some of these characteristics include:

- **Purpose Gives Direction and Clarity:** Purpose helps people determine what to pursue, what to avoid, and what deserves their time and their energy. Purpose eliminates aimless wandering and unnecessary distractions.

- **Purpose Creates Passion:** When people discover purpose, motivation increases, work becomes meaningful, sacrifice becomes worthwhile, and challenges become easier to endure because purpose fuels perseverance.

- **Purpose Produces Fulfillment:** Achievement alone does not satisfy the human soul. Purpose provides a deeper sense of significance. Many people are successful on the outside but empty on the inside because they have not connected with purpose.

- **Purpose Requires Stewardship:** Purpose is not automatic. It must be nurtured, developed, protected, and pursued. For instance, God gives an assignment, but we must choose whether to will walk in it.

- **Purpose Is Often Bigger Than the Individual:** Purpose often extends beyond personal benefit, impacting families, communities, nations, and future generations. The greatest purposes leave a legacy.

PASSION

Passion is the fire that fuels your pursuit of success. It is the deep inner drive that keeps you moving when everything around you tells you to stop. Passion is not just excitement; it is sustained enthusiasm rooted in purpose, because without passion, you will not have the energy to endure the long, hard journey toward greatness.

"Whatever you do, work at it with all your heart, as working for the Lord, not for human masters." Colossians 3:23 KJV

Passion turns ordinary effort into extraordinary impact. It is what makes you give more than is required, go further than is expected, and stay when others leave. When you are passionate about your purpose, work becomes worship, and sacrifice becomes sweet.

PLAN

Though God may give you the layout and instructions to accomplish something great when you pray, you must still plan strategically. When planning, you should always begin in advance, take important factors into account to avoid major obstacles, and allocate time and resources wisely. In fact, the Bible states:

"For which of you, intending to build a tower, sitteth not down first, and counteth the cost, whether he have sufficient to finish it?" Luke 14:28 KJV

Planning is the process of setting goals and selecting the most effective plan of action and the means to accomplish them. It is important to note that success does not require mere planning but planning that yields results. Effective planning anticipates future demands, evaluates current resources and limitations, accounts for challenges, assesses situations from every angle, and creates a series of activities to achieve desired outcomes.

It is a common saying that "If you fail to plan, you plan to fail." While many people pay no attention to this idea, it is a powerful principle and forms the foundation of success. Success does not simply happen by happenstance, nor does it happen overnight. Therefore, success must be intentional; a strategic plan of action is crucial. When you devise a plan to accomplish a goal, it establishes a sense of purpose and allows you to use your time meaningfully to create a pathway to success.

PLANNING FOR SUCCESS

Nonetheless, the Bible states: "There are many devices in a man's heart; nevertheless, the counsel of the LORD, that shall stand." Proverbs 19:21 KJV. Based on this verse, it is of the utmost importance to center and root your plans in Christ, as it is only the will of God that will stand when all else fails.

Planning is more than just a preparatory step; it is a crucial act because the steps taken in the preparatory stages ultimately determine the outcome of a goal. Planning provides the direction, organization, motivation, and drive required for success in any area of life. With effective planning, individuals may notice that challenges become avoidable because they were anticipated, and ways around those problems become clear on the path to success. By devoting time and effort to efficient planning, success is more likely. Adopting planning as a strategic weapon for success is critical to transforming visions into practical realities and goals into tangible accomplishments.

PREPARE

When attempting to achieve any level of success, preparation is essential. This includes not only physical preparation but also mental preparation. While hard work, talent, and dedication are important factors in the pursuit of success, the value of mental preparation cannot be overstated. The mind, with its vast power, can either be a catalyst for greatness, placing victory and success within arm's reach, or a roadblock to advancement, placing challenges and difficulties in the way. Mental preparation is just as important as physical planning, as it puts the mind in the headspace to not only attempt a plan but also achieve success.

Everything originates from within; thus, it is important to renew the mind. Cultivating a Godly mindset and developing resilience are part of the mental preparation needed for success. A Godly mindset can be fostered through many avenues, including but not limited to:

- Spending quality time in God's word
- Praying
- Fasting
- Engaging in consecration
- Limiting engagement in worldly activities
- Surrounding yourself with individuals possessing a Godly mindset

Additionally, when preparing for a goal, faith is required, but physical provisions are also needed, as the Bible states, "Faith without works is dead." If a plan is not as effective as needed, adjustments and improvements can be made to ensure its effectiveness. Notwithstanding, these adjustments should not be based on the carnal mind or made from a human perspective, but should be made in accordance with the will of God. When adjusting a devised plan, it is imperative that a person seek God for wisdom, knowledge, and understanding so that errors are not made in the process. With this in mind, preparing a plan can only be done with the help of God; therefore, continual, quality time in the presence of God is needed.

PLANNING FOR SUCCESS

PURSUE

Success does not come to those who wait; it comes to those who pursue. Pursuing means moving with intention, focus, and relentless effort toward your goal. It is not enough to have a dream; you must chase it. You must press in. You must not stop until you reach what God has set before you.

"Thou shalt search for me, if thou shall seek me with all thy heart." Jeremiah 29:13 KJV

Pursuing requires action. It requires discipline. It requires you to keep going when the path is unclear, results are slow, and obstacles are heavy. Pursuit is the bridge between potential and performance.

PRACTICE

If you devise a plan, you should practice it and put it into action. A plan should serve as a roadmap to achieving a goal and should therefore be followed carefully. If possible, you should never deviate from a strategically outlined plan. However, in some instances, a plan may appear impractical, and a more realistic and effective way to achieve a goal may emerge.

By setting clear, concise, and achievable goals, creating a structured schedule, holding oneself accountable, and, most importantly, seeking God's divine assistance, individuals can maintain their commitment to their pre-existing strategic plan of action. Staying true to a plan for success requires dedication, discipline, and the never-ceasing grace of God to accomplish what has been set forth. This is not an easy task, as we may not always see the benefits of following a plan and may even be compelled to give up. However, patience, one of the greatest hallmarks of success, is required of every individual who seeks to stay true to a devised plan. The Bible states, "but they that wait upon the LORD shall renew their strength; they shall mount up with wings as eagles; they shall run, and not be weary; and they shall walk, and not faint." Isaiah 40:31 KJV

The journey of practicing and staying true to a plan may be arduous and may require great sacrifice. However, the rewards of consistency, persistence, and perseverance are well worth it. Embracing the discipline of sticking to a plan not only leads to the achievement of goals but also fosters personal growth, development, and maturity, paving the way for perpetual cycles of success and prosperity in future endeavors.

PLANT A SEED

When pursuing any level of success, it is important to bring your sacrifice to the altar of prayer. Every endeavor should begin and end with God in mind. When your expectations are anchored in Him, He honors your devotion and alignment, and His favor is released over your efforts as you commit your plans to His will.

The reason God brings individuals out of poverty is not simply to make them look good, but because that individual has cut a covenant with God. One of the quickest ways to be delivered from the bondage and evil grip of poverty is to give your way out. Giving is a kingdom principle and a spiritual weapon that fights for you in the Realm of the Spirit. Out of an act of desperation, a noble sacrifice captures God's attention and makes Him more inclined to hearken to and answer our prayers. A sacrifice is an offering you physically can't afford to give, yet you are fully aware that you can't afford not to give it. There are several sacrifices, including but not limited to:

Preliminary Sacrifice/Vow Sacrifice: This refers to a blessing a person vows to God, even before receiving the blessing they are praying for (e.g., if God saves your child, you vow to give the child back to God). The problem, however, is that God records this vow. Thus, it is imperative to remain true to the vow and not renege on it.

The life of Hannah illustrates the utterance of a preliminary vow. Because she was barren, Hannah entered the temple and began to pray fervently before the face of God. She was so engaged in her prayer that the priest, Eli, believed she was intoxicated. He saw Hannah's lips moving, but could no longer understand the words leaving her mouth. Hannah took this prayer to another level by making a preliminary vow, promising God that if He granted her the desire of her heart, the ability to bear a child, she would give the child back to Him. Because of the extreme measures Hannah took, God inclined His ears to her prayer and granted her a son named Samuel. Nonetheless, it should be noted that Hannah stayed true to her vow and gave Samuel back to God.

Material/Physical Sacrifice: Additionally, Solomon gave twenty-two hundred (2,200) oxen and one hundred twenty thousand (120,000) sheep, and he gave so liberally that God saw fit to bless him. He was blessed beyond measure and became the wisest and wealthiest man known to man. Likewise, if you desire to be blessed by God, you should not be exacting and calculating in giving; instead, you should find joy in sowing liberally. Not only should you offer material sacrifices, but you should also offer yourself as a living sacrifice before God.

Living Sacrifice: This level of sacrifice is what we, as believers, are called to be. It involves pursuing holiness, righteousness, and truth daily. There is no need to sacrifice animals, because Jesus has already become the ultimate sacrifice. However, when we symbolically present a sacrifice by dying to our flesh and fulfilling Christ's desires, we ultimately enable our success.

When presenting ourselves as a living sacrifice unto God, it is also important to assume a posture of prayer. This posture signifies a constant state of prayer. Though this is not a popular perspective, we, as believers, are called to live in a continual posture of prayer, with our spirits positioned to hear and receive from God. To accomplish anything truly significant, one must remain sensitive to His voice, available for His use, and consistently aligned to receive His direction and guidance.

PRODUCE

True success is not measured by what you know, plan, or intend; it is measured by what you produce. This production refers to bringing forth and birthing results. It means output. It means bringing something tangible into existence that benefits others and fulfills your purpose. Potential without production is wasted. Passion without production is empty. Pursuit without production is futile.

Producing and bringing something forth is the final proof that you have walked in faith, done the work, and stayed true to your calling. It is the visible manifestation of everything you have prayed for, planned, practiced, and pursued. When you produce, you complete the cycle of success.

HOW TO HAVE TRUE SUCCESS IN YOUR NEW SEASON

Many people believe that success means having a good job, a nice car, fame, lots of money, and, of course, the accommodating "partner." Some people even dare to believe that partying or running with the "status quo" is what life is all about. None of these defines true success and are merely things you may attain as a result of becoming successful.

In fact, a drug dealer's idea of success may be measured by how many tons of drugs he has sold in his neighborhood, while disregarding how many young people he has destroyed. Likewise, a criminal may consider himself successful because he has robbed scores of people and accumulated enough wealth to live in a mansion near the beach. Yet despite his riches, he cannot move freely within the community and must constantly rely on armed security for protection. Becoming successful through illegal or selfish means can be short-lived and often leads to a life of misery.

True success can be achieved only with the help of God and maintained only through careful guidance from the Holy Spirit. People who live from day to day, without consulting God or seeking His divine will, move from one failing circumstance to another. Satan craftily convinces them that they are "self-made" masterminds who have cleverly engineered their life's accomplishments by their own power-driven mindset.

Jesus spoke vividly throughout the Scriptures about those who build their lives on false foundations. In Matthew 7:26–27, He described a foolish man who built his house on the sand. When the rains fell, the floods came, and the winds beat against that house, it collapsed because it lacked a solid foundation. In contrast, Jesus described a wise man who built his house on a rock. Though storms, floods, and fierce winds came against it, the house remained standing because it was firmly founded on the rock. This powerful illustration shows that true success is not determined by outward appearance or temporary achievements, but by the strength and stability of the foundation on which one's life is built.

Building or attempting to achieve any level of success without acknowledging or obtaining the blessing of the almighty God will only lead to a life of relentless struggle and failure. This is not God's divine plan for any of His children; He does not want anyone to suffer through a life of hardship.

PRACTICAL STEPS FOR TRUE SUCCESS

To truly succeed in life, several basic things must be put into practice. Some of these practices include:

- **Assess Your Relationship with God and Seek Him First.** Spend sacred time in prayer, meditation, and worship. Take time to examine the foundation of your Christian faith and know what you believe. This will be the season to unlock and engage the supernatural Realm of God. In this season, you must be led by the Spirit of God, not by your own intellect, because nothing will succeed by your own might or power. (Matthew 6:33; Zechariah 4:6)

- **Engage in daily spiritual declarations and affirmations.** They are an act of faith and alignment with God’s truth, and you attract what you consistently speak.

- **You should check your value system**: Who are you serving? What do you spend most of your time on?

- **Assess your sphere of influence**: Who is your spiritual mentor and prophetic coach? Who are you listening to and following? Over time, you absorb the mindset, the faith, the habits, and even the limitations of those you sit under. You become a sum total of who you listen to and follow.
- **Assess Your Past Successes and Failures.** Determine which people or habits are moving you closer to your goals and which are moving you further away.
- **"Spring Clean" Your Life.** Get rid of clutter. Hold on only to what is necessary. Cast away worry, stress, and anything that causes you unnecessary hardship. (Isaiah 26:3)
- **Forgive Quickly.** Forgiveness is one of the most difficult things for many people. However, we must remember that it frees us from any yoke of bitterness or resentment.
- **Love everyone.** Love is a powerful force in life. Show compassion toward others and demonstrate that you care. People never refuse or reject love. (1 John 4)
- **Give! Give! Give!** Make giving a habit by giving something every day. Offer compliments, encouragement, a smile, a helping hand, food, clothing, resources, or financial support whenever possible. No act of generosity is too small. Consistent giving cultivates a heart of compassion and opens the door to positive impact in others' lives. It is a proven principle that those who live generously often experience greater fulfillment, stronger relationships, and increased opportunities. As you sow into the lives of others, you activate the biblical law of sowing and reaping,

positioning yourself to receive a harvest in due season (Acts 20:35).

- **Discern What is Fake from What is Real.** Make sound decisions, and never make life-altering decisions based on temporary circumstances. You cannot fix a problem at the same level at which it started; be prepared to rise above your storm by activating the Law of Cause and Effect, which holds that every action has an equal and opposite reaction.

- **Seek God for His Divine Will and Wisdom.** Do this in every area of your life. The Bible teaches that wisdom is the principal thing; therefore, seek understanding and discern the season God has ordained for you. This is a time to embrace your God-given gifts, creativity, and opportunities.

- **Seek Financial Freedom.** Make every effort to become debt-free and practice wise financial stewardship. Wealth acquisition, when guided by God's principles, can be a powerful tool for fulfilling His purpose. Do not wait for opportunities to come to you; be proactive, create value, and develop systems of trade and investment. As you do, you position yourself to prosper and walk in God's provision, remembering that it is the Father's good pleasure to give you the Kingdom (Luke 12:32).

- **Discover Your True Purpose.** Not what someone else wants you to do. Find a cause that's worth your time or investment and support it.

- **Choose Your Friends and Know Your Enemies.** Jesus cannot cast out your friends; he can only cast out your enemies. Your true friends will push you closer to your destiny, while your enemies will try to drive you away from it.

- **Discover The Origin, Source, and Root.** Apply them to everything that comes into your life. You must be able to discover: (The origin is the foundation from which something came. The source is what fuels it or gives it strength. The root is what holds it in place.)

- **Conduct Daily Inspections.** Assess what type of fruit you are bearing. Every tree bears fruit after its kind in its season, and every season is governed by time. Jesus said each tree is known by its fruit. (Luke 6:44, Matthew 12:33).

- **Journal Your Journey.** It is well known that we commit more to long-term memory when we write. Once you have sought God for direction, removed the clutter from your life, and begun the quest to seek out the divine will and wisdom of God in this season, write your future plans and put every measure in place to accomplish them (Habakkuk 2:2).

- **Remain Flexible and Embrace Change.** Every season of life requires adjustment, growth, and sometimes a change of direction. Do not become so attached to the past that you miss what God is doing in the present. Be willing to learn, adapt, and follow God's leading, even when it takes you beyond your comfort zone. Remember that God often uses change as a tool for transformation and advancement. Stay teachable, remain faithful, and trust Him to guide your steps into His perfect plan (Isaiah 43:19; Proverbs 3:5-6).

Regardless of where you may find yourself right now, please know that you are not a failure. If you have failed, it is never too late to try again!

GODLINESS WITH CONTENTMENT

In a world that often values material possessions, wealth, and personal gain above all else, Joshua 1:8 is a clear reminder that not all success is good success. When we prioritize our relationship with God, we can experience peace and contentment that cannot be found anywhere else. When we seek God for success rather than the world, we can rest assured that true good success, one of great longevity, shall be granted unto us.

THE WINNER'S MINDSET

"But thanks be to God, which gives us the victory through our Lord Jesus Christ." 1 Corinthians 15:57 KJV

CHAPTER FIVE

HOW YOU SEE WHAT YOU SEE

Though aspiring to succeed is a noteworthy act, it should be noted that success is not solely a one-time event but a mindset. The mind is one of the most powerful tools a person possesses, as it shapes the entire essence of a person's identity. The mind is a region of the soul, housed within the human body, and shapes how we act, think, feel, and ultimately perceive life. Our entire way of living is based on the premises of the mind, and therefore, our victory and success depend on our mindset, which heavily influences our perception.

A person's perception is how they see the world. For example, a glass containing fifty percent (50%) water can be viewed through two different lenses: pessimism or optimism. Through the lens of pessimism, a person will perceive the glass as half empty, viewing life darkly and seeing the negative in everything. On the contrary, optimistic individuals are hopeful and see the positive in everything. As a result, these individuals will perceive the glass as half-full.

Although perception is a common principle of life, it is also an essential component that must be continually renewed, as the Bible vividly states, *"For as he thinketh in his heart, so is he:"* Thus, the mind must be kept in spiritual alignment with Christ and maintained daily.

"For as he thinketh in his heart, so is he:"
Proverbs 23:7 KJV

PLANNING FOR SUCCESS

Before any level of success can be achieved, and before you can win in any area of life, the battle in the mind must be won first. Contrary to popular belief, the ongoing battle is not against flesh and blood. Rather, it involves demonic strongholds rising against the mind, seeking to undermine the believer's well-being and ultimately destroy that individual's life. A demonic stronghold is a fortified place and alludes to a deviant, anti-Christ belief system that leads the possessor to believe things about themselves that God has not spoken. ***(See more in Chapter 2)***

WINNERS MAKE IT HAPPEN

It was once said that there are three basic groups of people, and you are likely to fall into one of them. Either you will be in a group of people who are always about to make something happen, who are making something happen, or who are wondering what just happened! Winners "Make things happen!" They have an uncanny grace upon their lives that turns a no into a yes; moves their files from the bottom to the top; turns their losses into triumphs; and brings all things together for their good. (Romans 8:28)

In some instances, it may be a coincidence, a supernatural favor, or a special grace. However, I propose that a winner's mindset approaches life deliberately. Their moves are strategic, calculated, and cleverly orchestrated to turn the tide of favor in their favor. They are prepared to fight a little harder, talk a little longer, go the extra mile, or put in just a little more effort to get the job done.

Many individuals claim to have faith but offer only words about what they perceive as faith. True faith in God ignites action. If you know that God is calling you to do something, you must put your hands and feet to work. In this regard, your faith is demonstrated when the odds are stacked against you, yet you overcome every demonic resistance or obstacle and get the job done.

At the end of the day, the only true mark of a winner is the one who gets the job done. I firmly believe that the glory is in the finish. The Word of God admonishes that "better is the end of a thing than the beginning" because the end either confirms or disproves what was perceived at the beginning. We are also taught that whatever a thing's origin is, its conclusion or outcome will reflect that origin.

God has given you the ability to manifest what He has placed within you. He is deeply interested in your visions and dreams coming to pass because He gave them to you to manifest in the right season, at the right time, and in the right place, all in an effort to fulfill His divine purpose. If we are ever to come into divine alignment with the purpose God has called us to fulfill, we must possess more than "faith talk", demonstrating and "walking out" our faith every day.

GATES: DIVINE OPPORTUNITIES

Those in the valley of deliberation often fail to achieve a breakthrough. Gates exist because God seeks to give individuals prophetic signs that it is time to change, turn around, and achieve a breakthrough. In 2 Kings, the four lepers said among themselves that if they remained outside the gate, they would surely die. Thus, they made a conscious decision to enter the city in search of their breakthrough (healing), even though they were not legally permitted to do so because of their disease.

The gate represents an opportunity. However, it goes beyond being merely an opportunity. It is a point of decision, transition, and divine access. It is a place where destiny can shift and where faith must overcome fear, hesitation, and limitation. Gates symbolize moments when God calls a person to move from stagnation to progress, from bondage to freedom, and from lack to fulfillment. Those who discern the significance of the gate and boldly move through it position themselves to experience transformation, favor, and supernatural breakthrough.

"And a certain man lame from his mother's womb was carried, whom they laid daily at the gate of the temple which is called Beautiful, to ask alms of them that entered into the temple;"
Acts 3:2 KJV

The lame man mentioned in this verse was at a beautiful gate, yet he faced an ugly situation. Peter then appeared and demonstrated the power given to him by God to command the man to rise and walk. This man undoubtedly walked because of the name of Jesus, and he also walked because Peter, by faith, commanded him to do so. Similarly, we must not only be a "talker" but also a demonstrator, as this will ultimately push us through the gates of opportunity.

PERSISTENCY IN SUCCESS

Success requires persistence. Persistence means continually trying, seeking, and knocking, despite the enemy's plots, schemes, and darts. The road to success is not paved with gold but with trials, tribulations, and severe persecution. Therefore, without persistence and faith in God, no level of success can be achieved.

A prime example of achieving victory through persistence is found in the parable of the widow and the unjust judge. In this account, the Bible recounts a widow pleading before a judge who had no respect, honor, or fear of God. While this would instill fear in the average Christian, prompting them to give up because the judge regarded neither God nor man, the widow is portrayed as persistently going before the judge with unwavering faith. Eventually, the widow achieved victory when the judge decided to avenge her, simply because of her persistence.

"[1] And he spake a parable unto them to this end, that men ought always to pray, and not to faint; [2] Saying, There was in a city a judge, which feared not God, neither regarded man: [3] And there was a widow in that city; and she came unto him, saying, Avenge me of mine adversary. [4] And he would not for a while: but afterward he said within himself, Though I fear not God, nor regard man; [5] Yet because this widow troubleth me, I will avenge her, lest by her continual coming she weary me."
Luke 18:1-5 KJV

Likewise, God, the Just Judge, will answer your prayers and grant you the desires of your heart in accordance with His will when persistent faith is present.

PLANNING FOR SUCCESS

On the journey to success, it is common to lose friends, family, and even those closest to the heart, as God sometimes removes people from our lives to prepare us for what lies ahead, and to save us the pain of being surrounded by foes. In fact, no one who has ever climbed to the mountain of greatness has made it there without losing friends or loved ones along the way.

SECRETS OF SUCCESSFUL PEOPLE

Successful people understand the importance of self-discovery. They do not allow outward appearances, public opinions, or temporary circumstances to define them. Instead, they take the time to seek understanding concerning their identity, purpose, and divine assignment in life.

On the road to success, you must:

- *Discover Your True Self.*
- *Look Beyond External Appearances and Search Within.*
- *Ask Yourself:* (Who am I? Why was I born? What purpose do I serve on the earth? Why did God place me in this body and not another?)

God made you, beloved, exactly as you are. He created you with intention and placed you precisely where you need to be. You are not someone else, nor are you somewhere else without purpose. God crafted your identity and your place in this world with purpose. The sooner you embrace who you are, as God created you, the sooner you will unlock your full potential. You'll realize that God has a specific reason for your existence. Your task is to discover that purpose and pursue it. God wants you to succeed!

Many people are unsure whether God wants them to be successful. They often doubt that God desires success for them personally, even if they can accept it for others. They see their neighbors thriving and blessed yet struggle to believe it can happen for them. They think, "I was born into a certain situation; we don't have much money, and maybe if I had attended a different school or had a better job, I would be successful."

As a result, they allow their background, limitations, and past experiences to shape their expectations for the future. Instead of seeing themselves through God's eyes, they measure their potential by their circumstances. However, God is not limited by where you came from, what you lack, or the obstacles before you. He specializes in taking ordinary people from difficult situations and raising them to places of purpose, influence, and blessing. Your success is not determined by your environment alone but by your willingness to believe God, obey His instructions, and pursue the purpose He has placed within you.

Most people spend their entire lives searching for happiness and striving for success. They ask me why this is the case and why it often doesn't work out. My answer is simple, and I want everyone to focus on:

Success is not defined by what others possess, nor is it measured by the standards of this world.

Contrary to popular belief, true success is not found in education, status, or material wealth. A person may accumulate great riches and still live unfulfilled, while another may attain impressive credentials yet never walk in the purpose for which they were created. True success begins with the transformation of the mind and the alignment of the heart with the will of God.

It is discovered when a person embraces the divine purpose, calling, and assignment uniquely entrusted to them by God. Success is not merely about achieving goals; it is about becoming who God created you to be and faithfully fulfilling His purpose for your life.

Success is not about material possessions or their absence. Many people who started with nothing have achieved great success in life. Some are considered successful despite coming from humble beginnings. Success is also not limited by physical conditions; some have achieved remarkable success with only one hand or without legs.

Your current position in life is determined by the reality you step into. Prayer will help you fully reveal what God has placed within you. Once you discover something great within you and begin to recognize and celebrate it, you will begin to perfect it. As you do this, others will begin to recognize your success.

MY IDEA OF SUCCESS

The way I view success is somewhat different from the way most people view it. I noted the life of a man by the name of Jeremiah Lanphier (1809–1898), a successful New York businessman who left the business world to serve as a lay minister.

In September 1857, Lanphier began inviting businessmen to a daily noonday prayer meeting. On the first day, he prayed alone for thirty minutes before anyone arrived. By the end of the meeting, only six people had attended. What seemed like a small beginning soon became the *Fulton Street Prayer Revival*. As the financial Panic of 1857 spread across

America, thousands turned to God. Prayer meetings multiplied throughout New York City and across the nation. Within months, more than 10,000 businessmen were gathering daily for prayer, and historians estimate that hundreds of thousands came to faith during the revival.

What makes Lanphier's story remarkable is that he was not a famous preacher. He was simply a businessman who obeyed God. Today, few people remember his financial success, but history remembers the spiritual impact he made. His life teaches us that success is not measured by what we accumulate, but by our obedience to God and the lives we influence for His Kingdom.

Jeremiah Lanphier was not known for wealth, fame, or a large ministry. He is remembered because he answered God's call to pray. Through one noon prayer meeting, he helped ignite the Fulton Street Prayer Revival, a movement that brought spiritual awakening to America and demonstrated the extraordinary power of ordinary believers who pray.

PEOPLE THE WORLD CALL SUCCESSFUL

The following are some of the things I noticed about people who are seen as successful in the eyes of the world.

MOTHER TERESA

***Mother Teresa*:** Born on April 26, 1910, she was a Roman Catholic nun and missionary who devoted her life to serving the poorest and sickest among society, most notably in Kolkata, India. In 1950, she founded the Missionaries of Charity, a religious order committed to caring for those living in poverty. Her selfless work earned her the Nobel Peace Prize in 1979, and in 2016, the Catholic Church declared her a saint. Though she lived with almost nothing in the way of personal possessions, she stands as perhaps the most celebrated humanitarian of the twentieth century, a life shaped by a remarkable set of qualities, including:

- **Faith:** Mother Teresa's work was built on her belief in God and her trust that her service was unto Him. This gave her the strength to persevere, even in the midst of great difficulty.
- **Passion and Compassion for People:** Mother Teresa had a deep love for humanity and a sincere desire to help those in need. Her compassion led her to consistently serve the poor, the sick, and the forgotten.
- **A burden to see others succeed:** She wanted others to experience dignity, healing, and hope. Her life was not centered on personal gain but on lifting up those whom society had overlooked.
- **Selflessness:** She lived for the needs of others, often putting their comfort above her own. Her life demonstrated what it means to give without seeking recognition.
- **Humility:** She never built her life around status or possessions. Instead, she embraced simplicity and served quietly.
- **Servant leadership:** Her leadership was defined not by the pursuit of authority, but by a commitment to serve. She embodied the truth that genuine greatness is measured by how faithfully we meet the needs of those around us.

- **Sacrifice:** She devoted her time, energy, and comfort to support others. Her life was marked by a willingness to endure hardship for a greater purpose.

VINCE LOMBARDI

Vince Lombardi: Born June 11, 1913, is considered one of the greatest football coaches of all time. Born to Italian immigrant parents, his rise to greatness was shaped by several defining qualities:

- **Faith**: Lombardi's love for God was central to his life, praying regularly with his players and earning a medal for "Distinction in service to God through excellence in his chosen profession," a day he called the greatest of his life.
- **Passion & Desire to Excel:** His deep love for football and relentless drive to win fueled his dedication and earned him his first head coaching opportunity straight out of university.
- **Discipline & Work Ethic:** Shaped by his college coaches, Lombardi embraced hard work and discipline, living by the belief that "winners never quit, and quitters never win."
- **Leadership & Trust**: His ability to inspire confidence in players pushed them to perform at their best.
- **Winning Mindset & Resilience:** Lombardi viewed winning as the only option, famously declaring, "Winning isn't everything, it's the only thing." Even in adversity, he never quit.
- **Strategic Thinking:** His deep knowledge of the game and opposing players allowed him to gain a competitive edge, most notably transforming the Green Bay Packers into a dynasty that captured five (5) NFL championships.

POWERED FROM THE SECRET PLACE

"The effectual fervent prayer of a righteous man availeth much." James 5:16 KJV

CHAPTER SIX

THE POWER OF RADICAL PRAYER

Proseiche (gk): To pray, to come into a relationship with God, and to adopt a lifestyle of prayer. This is mentioned over 400 times in scripture.

Prayer is central to the life of a Christian, and when Christians lack a lifestyle of prayer, they tend to be controlled by others' prayers and atmospheres. Many Christians make the mistake of praying only when their lives seem to be going well. However, your prayers should not be based on your circumstances or your present state of affairs. They should be based on a consistent relationship with God, not on the roller coaster of your emotions.

Many people do not receive an answer to their prayers because they lack sustenance, consistency, and persistence. Your prayer life and relationship with God should never be based on how you feel; rather, it should be based on a spiritual belief system where you understand that it is a mechanism that God has given unto you to achieve success and have access to Him and everything He owns.

Prayer is the creation of a system that God Himself has established to give people an opportunity to have access to Him. Prayer is born out of a love relationship with God, and when prayer is mastered, it gives you a spiritual advantage. However, because many people do not believe this, they become disadvantaged and don't pursue prayer.

PLANNING FOR SUCCESS

The mystery of prayer is that it must be pursued, and the only way to pursue it is to first desire it. In addition to living a consecrated life, demonic strongholds can also be demolished in prayer. During times of prayer, it is crucial to pray against demonic strongholds. However, a stronghold cannot be cast out, because it involves thoughts that remain with a person and cannot leave. Instead, a demonic stronghold should be cast down, or the demonic strongman holding the stronghold in place should be cast out and removed from its assignment. After this is done, the Word of God should be employed, and you should replace every negative thought about yourself with what God has spoken concerning you.

The way to hear God is to pick His mouth and "provoke" Him.

There are many ranks of demons that exist to stop and hinder an individual's progress and development. For example, many individuals start their journey to greatness but never achieve success. These demonic ranks include not only principalities but also powers, rulers of the darkness of this world, and spiritual wickedness in high places. For those in the kingdom of this world, these demonic ranks are not an issue, as they are of their kingdom. However, they pose a threat to those in the kingdom of God, as these demonic powers fight against those who are not a part of their kingdom. We, as believers, must begin to exercise judgment over our adversaries and begin powerfully manifesting the gifts God has given us.

Although some individuals may have been delivered, meaning a demon has been completely exorcised from them, they may still experience symptoms of that demon's presence. This is largely because God waits for a decree to go forth from us to completely stop the demon's function. Jesus not only gives power to His prophets and apostles but also to the body of Christ, as the blood of Jesus gives us the legal right and authority to stop the enemy in its tracks. The same power that resurrected Jesus from the dead is the very power God has given to those who believe in Him.

When prayer becomes a lifestyle:

- An altar should be raised.
- Cleansing, washing, purging must be done.
- Sanctification must be pursued.
- Consecration must ultimately be practiced.

PROPHETIC PRAYER CODES FOR SUCCESS

A prayer code is used to achieve desired results. The following are prayer codes for success, and when used correctly, they can grant you access into the realm of success, opening doors that may have seemed unreachable. One important point to understand is that just as keys provide access to doors, so too do prayer codes act as secret weapons. It weaponizes and empowers you to accomplish things you might not ordinarily be able to do, unlocking opportunities beyond your natural ability.

Some of the prayer codes for success that I have discovered over the years are as follows:

- **Prayer Code of Wisdom**: Using divine wisdom instead of relying solely on human understanding.

- **Prayer Code of Meditation**: Intentionally focus your mind on God's Word and presence to gain clarity, revelation, and inner transformation.
- **Prayer Code of Consistency**: Praying regularly without giving up.
- **Prayer Code of Persistency**: Presenting matters to God and relentlessly pursuing them in prayer.
- **Prayer Code of Perseverance**: Remaining steadfast despite challenges or delays.
- **Prayer Code of Resilience:** Bouncing back from difficulties with faith strengthened.
- **Prayer Code of Timing:** Discerning God's timing and knowing when to move, wait, or act.
- **Prayer Code of Attention to Detail**: Being spiritually sensitive and recognizing that even small instructions from God matter.
- **Prayer Code of Alignment**: Bringing your thoughts, desires, and actions into agreement with God's will.
- **Prayer Code of Visions**: Receiving and praying through divine revelations about your future and purpose.
- **Prayer Code of Dreams**: Understanding and interpreting God-given dreams for direction.
- **Prayer Code of Imagination:** Allowing your mind to be shaped by God's promises and seeing beyond the natural.

- **Prayer Code of Activation:** Acting on what God reveals to turn prayer into results.

- **Prayer Code of Casting Down Strongholds**: Destroying negative thoughts and spiritual barriers that oppose the truth.

- **Prayer Code of Access**: Recognizing and exercising your spiritual authority to approach God and operate in His promises.

- **Prayer Code of Asking**: Presenting requests to God with faith and clarity.

- **Prayer Code of Seeking**: Diligently pursuing God for understanding and a deeper relationship.

- **Prayer Code of Knocking**: Persisting in prayer until doors open and answers come.

- **Prayer Code of Visualization**: Seeing through faith what God has promised and aligning your prayers with it.

- **Prayer Code of Waiting**: Trusting God while answers are prepared.

- **Prayer Code of Patience**: Maintaining faith over time despite delays.

- **Prayer Code of Fasting**: Denying the flesh to strengthen the spirit and heighten sensitivity to God.

- **Prayer Code of Faith**: Trusting God fully, even without visible evidence.

- **Prayer Code of Spiritual Warfare**: Engaging in prayer to overcome spiritual opposition.

- **Prayer Code of Contending**: Earnestly pressing in prayer for God's will to be established.
- **Prayer Code of Intensity**: Praying with urgency and deep passion when needed.
- **Prayer Code of Endurance**: Continuing in prayer for extended periods without quitting.
- **Prayer Code of Sacrificial Giving**: Giving beyond comfort as an act of worship.
- **Prayer Code of Peace:** Maintaining inner calm and trust in God regardless of circumstances.
- **Prayer Code of Serving**: Embracing humility through service, because greatness comes through serving others.
- **Prayer Code of Honor**: Valuing and respecting what God has established; honoring attracts blessing, as seen in the life of Elijah.
- **Prayer Code of the Fruits of the Spirit**: Developing love, joy, peace, patience, kindness, goodness, faithfulness, gentleness, and self-control.
- **Prayer Code of Righteousness**: Living in right standing with God.
- **Prayer Code of Integrity**: Walking in honesty and moral integrity.
- **Prayer Code of Holiness**: Living a consecrated life; a key spiritual virtue that governs success.
- **Prayer Code of Discernment**: Recognizing what is of God and making spiritually wise decisions.

- **Prayer Code of Humility:** Remaining humble and dependent on God.
- **Prayer Code of Rest**: Trusting God enough to rest, knowing He is working on your behalf.
- **Prayer Code of Sobriety**: Walking in clear-mindedness, self-control, and spiritual alertness.
- **Prayer Code of Planning**: Seeking God for strategy and direction.

SUCCEEDING THROUGH SERVING

Did you realize that most people go through life looking to be served rather than to serve? I believe one of the greatest ingredients for success is becoming a servant of God and of others, willing to serve in the kingdom of God. In His discussion with His disciples, Jesus clearly pointed out that if anyone was going to be great in the kingdom, they should assume the position of a servant.

He was demonstrating a principle He Himself was embodying. He laid aside His deity and took on the form of a servant, becoming obedient unto death, even the death of the cross. Therefore, it is my opinion that true success is found in finding someone greater than yourself and positioning yourself to serve them.

Mother Teresa stands as a perfect example of this kind of life. One could argue that she died with very few personal possessions, yet she was among the wealthiest women who ever lived, not because of what she owned but because of what she invested in humanity. The world often measures wealth by what a person accumulates. God often measures wealth by what a person contributes. Mother Teresa owned no mansion, held no stock portfolio, drove no luxury vehicles, and left no personal fortune. Yet her influence spanned continents, her work touched millions of lives, and her legacy continues to inspire compassion, generosity, and service around the world.

SUCCEEDING THROUGH SACRIFICIAL GIVING

To be successful, you must be a giver, and giving, particularly of a sacrificial nature, must become one of your key gifts. Most successful people are big on giving. Throughout Scripture and across the world, we see people who sow and give to charitable and noteworthy organizations, and this is exactly how we should live our lives.

Unfortunately, most people live expecting to receive, but true success is built on giving, not getting. The word of God explicitly states, "It is more blessed to give than to receive" (Acts 20:35). Jesus demonstrated this by giving up His glory, becoming a servant, and pouring out His life on the cross. He further explained the success that comes from giving, saying: "Give, and it shall be given unto you; good measure, pressed down, shaken together, and running over" (Luke 6:38). When you give freely, God blesses you abundantly, not just for you to keep, but to give again. The more you release, the more you truly possess.

In **Matthew 19:21**, Jesus meets a young man who asks Him how to become successful. Jesus tells him: ***"If thou will be perfect, go and sell that thou havest, and give to the poor, and thou shall have treasure in heaven: and come and follow me." (Matthew 19:21 KJV)***

When the young man heard this, he went away sorrowful because he had great possessions. He trusted in his riches more than in the call to give and follow Jesus. This shows that some people cannot succeed because they trust in what they have rather than in what God can do through them when they give.

SUCCEEDING THROUGH FORGIVENESS

The next step on the road to success is forgiving the perpetrator. Many refuse to do this, thinking of all the pain they've experienced because of their perpetrator. This process can cause extreme emotional agony in victims' lives, as many believe that it is the perpetrator who truly owes them forgiveness. While this may be true, the forgiveness process is for your benefit, as holding a grudge keeps you from growing and entering a state of perpetual freedom. Contrary to popular belief, forgiving a person does not mean that you must go to lunch with them or even converse with that person. Although this step may even involve shedding tears, it is an extremely important part of the deliverance process for an embattled mind.

Today, many "preachers" have begun preaching about the grace of God, and while the church is in the dispensation of grace, it is not an occasion to sin. However, grace refers to God's merciful pardon and love extended to us, and should therefore be an incentive for every believer to turn away from sin and toward a lifestyle of holiness and consecration. Grace is not a cover-up for sin but a deliverance from sin, symbolizing the unmerited, undeserved opportunity from God to change one's life and to turn to a lifestyle of holiness, righteousness, truth, and consecration.

PURPOSE OF FASTING

Fasting is a means of humbling oneself before God. In Psalm 35:13, David says, *"But as for me, when they were sick, my clothing was sackcloth: I humbled my soul with fasting; and my prayer returned into mine own bosom."* This verse highlights that fasting is a way to humble oneself and earnestly seek God's face. It demonstrates repentance, dependence on God, and a desire for His intervention.

Fasting is also a powerful tool in spiritual warfare. In Mark 9:29, Jesus says, *"And he said unto them, This kind can come forth by nothing, but by prayer and fasting."* This statement underscores that certain spiritual battles and strongholds can be overcome only through the combined power of prayer and fasting. It shows that fasting intensifies our prayers and equips us to face and defeat spiritual opposition.

Fasting helps believers receive divine guidance and wisdom. In Acts 13:2-3, it is recorded, *"As they ministered to the Lord, and fasted, the Holy Ghost said, Separate me Barnabas and Saul for the work whereunto I have called them. And when they had fasted and prayed, and laid their hands on them, they sent them away."* This passage illustrates that fasting, combined with prayer, leads to clear direction from the Holy Spirit, enabling believers to understand and follow God's will.

Fasting provides spiritual strength and clarity. Isaiah 58:6 declares, "*Is not this the fast that I have chosen? to loose the bands of wickedness, to undo the heavy burdens, and to let the oppressed go free, and that ye break every yoke?"* This verse emphasizes that true fasting can break spiritual strongholds, release burdens, and bring freedom to those who are oppressed. It reveals that fasting has a profound impact on spiritual dynamics.

Fasting brings rewards from God. In Matthew 6:17-18, Jesus instructs, *"But thou, when thou fastest, anoint thine head, and wash thy face; That thou appear not unto men to fast, but unto thy Father which is in secret: and thy Father, which seeth in secret, shall reward thee openly."* This passage teaches that fasting should be done with the right motives, not for show, but for God. It assures believers that God sees their fasting in secret and rewards them openly.

Jesus Himself set an example of fasting. In Matthew 4:1-2, it is written, *"Then was Jesus led up of the Spirit into the wilderness to be tempted of the devil. And when he had fasted forty days and forty nights, he was afterward an hungred."* Jesus' forty-day fast before beginning His public ministry shows the importance of fasting for spiritual preparation and empowerment. It shows that fasting equips believers to face and overcome trials and temptations.

To walk effectively in the discipline of fasting, believers must approach it with the right heart and motives. Joel 2:12-13 encourages, *"Therefore also now, saith the LORD, turn ye even to me with all your heart, and with fasting, and with weeping, and with mourning: And rend your heart, and not your garments, and turn unto the LORD your God: for he is gracious and merciful, slow to anger, and of great kindness, and repenteth him of the evil."* This passage calls for sincere repentance and heartfelt devotion in fasting, reminding believers of God's grace and mercy.

SUCCEEDING BY FASTING

Fasting is a powerful spiritual discipline that believers can use to draw closer to God, seek His guidance, and gain victory in their spiritual battles. The Bible provides numerous examples and teachings on the importance and benefits of fasting. Winning by fasting means engaging in this spiritual discipline with sincerity and purpose. Fasting humbles us, intensifies our prayers, and provides divine guidance and strength. It is a means of seeking God's intervention in our lives and spiritual battles. By following the biblical principles of fasting, we, as believers, can experience profound spiritual breakthroughs and victories. Let us, therefore, embrace the discipline of fasting, knowing that through it, we can draw closer to God and win in our spiritual journey.

THE IMPORTANCE OF STUDYING THE WORD

Studying the Word of God is crucial for spiritual growth and maturity. In 2 Timothy 2:15, it says, *"Study to shew thyself approved unto God, a workman that needeth not to be ashamed, rightly dividing the word of truth."* This verse encourages believers to be diligent in their study of Scripture, aiming to understand and interpret the Word accurately. Through studying, believers can deepen their knowledge of God and His will.

The Word of God is a powerful weapon in spiritual battles. In Ephesians 6:17, the Bible describes the Word as *"the sword of the Spirit, which is the word of God."* This imagery highlights the offensive power of Scripture in combating spiritual forces. Jesus Himself demonstrated this when He was tempted by Satan in the wilderness. By quoting

Scripture, He resisted temptation, showing us the power of God's Word to overcome trials.

"It is written, Man shall not live by bread alone, but by every word that proceedeth out of the mouth of God." Matthew 4:4 KJV

The Word of God provides guidance and wisdom for life's decisions. Psalm 119:105 says, *"Thy word is a lamp unto my feet, and a light unto my path."* This verse illustrates how Scripture illuminates our path, guiding us through the complexities of life. By studying the Word, believers can gain divine wisdom and direction, ensuring their steps align with God's will.

The Word of God has the power to transform lives. Hebrews 4:12 declares, *"For the word of God is quick, and powerful, and sharper than any two-edged sword, piercing even to the dividing asunder of soul and spirit, and of the joints and marrow, and is a discerner of the thoughts and intents of the heart."* This passage emphasizes the penetrating and transformative power of Scripture, which can discern and change the deepest parts of our being. Through regular study and application of the Word, believers can experience profound spiritual transformation.

Quoting Scripture strengthens faith. Romans 10:17 says, *"So then faith cometh by hearing, and hearing by the word of God."* This verse shows that faith is built and strengthened by hearing and internalizing the Word of God. By consistently quoting and meditating on Scripture, we can strengthen our faith and stand firm on God's promises.

PLANNING FOR SUCCESS

SUCCEEDING BY STUDYING THE WORD AND QUOTING SCRIPTURES

Studying the Word of God and quoting Scriptures are fundamental practices for a victorious Christian life. The Bible emphasizes the importance of engaging deeply with God's Word, through which we gain wisdom, overcome challenges, and fulfill God's purposes. A dedicated and disciplined approach to Scripture enables believers to receive strength and guidance. By meditating on and quoting God's Word, we build our faith and experience transformation in our spiritual journey. Let us, therefore, immerse ourselves in the Scriptures, knowing that through them, we can truly win.

SUCCEEDING BY MEDITATION AND REST

Meditation and rest are essential to a victorious Christian life. The Bible emphasizes meditating on God's Word and finding rest in Him. Through these practices, believers can experience spiritual growth, stability, and prosperity. Winning through meditation and rest requires a disciplined focus on God's Word and solace in His presence. Meditation brings blessings, stability, and prosperity. Resting in God brings peace, strength, and renewal. By following the biblical principles of meditation and rest, we can experience victory and transformation in our spiritual journey. Let us, therefore, embrace meditating on God's Word and resting in His promises, knowing that through these, we can truly win.

Meditation on God's Word brings immense blessings. Psalm 1:1-3 declares, "*Blessed is the man that walketh not in the counsel of the ungodly, nor standeth in the way of sinners, nor sitteth in the seat of the scornful. But his delight is in the law of the LORD; and in his law doth he meditate day and night. And he shall be like a tree planted by the rivers of water, that bringeth forth his fruit in his season; his leaf also shall not wither; and whatsoever he doeth shall prosper."* This passage highlights that those who meditate on God's law consistently are blessed, fruitful, and prosperous. Meditation anchors believers, making them steadfast and resilient like a deeply rooted tree.

Meditating on Scripture fosters spiritual growth and understanding. Joshua 1:8 instructs, *"This book of the law shall not depart out of thy mouth; but thou shalt meditate therein day and night, that thou mayest observe to do according to all that is written therein: for then thou shalt make thy way prosperous, and then thou shalt have good success."* This verse emphasizes the importance of continuous meditation on God's Word, promising success and prosperity to those who diligently engage in it. By meditating on Scripture, believers internalize God's principles, which guide their actions and decisions.

Resting in God is essential to spiritual and physical well-being. In Matthew 11:28-29, Jesus invites us, saying, "*Come unto me, all ye that labour and are heavy laden, and I will give you rest. Take my yoke upon you, and learn of me; for I am meek and lowly in heart: and ye shall find rest unto your souls.*" This invitation underscores that true rest is found in Christ. By coming to Him and learning from Him, we can experience rest and renewal for our souls.

Meditation and rest in God bring peace that transcends circumstances. Isaiah 26:3 assures us, *"Thou wilt keep him in perfect peace, whose mind is stayed on thee: because he trusteth in thee."* This verse underscores that keeping our minds on God through meditation fosters perfect peace. Trusting in God and resting in His promises shields our hearts from anxiety and turmoil.

Meditation on God's Word and resting in Him provide strength for life's challenges. Psalm 46:10 reminds us, "*Be still, and know that I am God: I will be exalted among the heathen, I will be exalted in the earth.*" This call to stillness and recognition of God's sovereignty encourages believers to pause, reflect, and draw strength from the knowledge of God's power and presence. Being still before God allows believers to recharge and gain a fresh perspective.

Jesus exemplified the practice of meditation and rest. Mark 1:35 records, *"And in the morning, rising up a great while before day, he went out, and departed into a solitary place, and there prayed."* Jesus often withdrew to solitary places to meditate and pray, setting an example for believers. His practice of seeking solitude for communion with the Father underscores the importance of intentional meditation and rest. To walk in meditation and rest, we, as believers, must begin to prioritize quiet time with God and His Word.

"O how love I thy law! it is my meditation all the day."
Psalm 119:97 KJV

SPIRITUAL INTELLIGENCE

"Now faith is the substance of things hoped for, the evidence of things not seen." Hebrews 11:1 KJV

CHAPTER SEVEN

FORCE OF FAITH

The force of faith begins with trusting God. Scripture reminds us to "trust in the Lord," and again declares, "They that trust in the Lord shall be as Mount Zion." Trusting God is where you should stand as an individual. Some trust in horses, and some trust in chariots, but true success comes from trusting the Lord.

"Trust in the LORD with all thine heart; and lean not unto thine own understanding. In all thy ways acknowledge him, and he shall direct thy paths." Proverbs 3:5–6 KJV

"They that trust in the LORD shall be as mount Zion, which cannot be removed, but abideth for ever." Psalm 125:1 KJV

"Some trust in chariots, and some in horses: but we will remember the name of the LORD our God." Psalm 20:7 KJV

Attempting to succeed in life without faith is an absolute waste of time. Faith is required to win in any area of your life. Faith is having absolute confidence in God. It is the assurance that by the grace of God, you will accomplish what you desire to achieve.

"Now the just shall live by faith: but if any man draw back, my soul shall have no pleasure in him. But we are not of them who draw back unto perdition; but of them that believe to the saving of the soul." Hebrews 10:38-39 KJV

PLANNING FOR SUCCESS

> ***Winning by faith says you have already won!***

Winning by faith is simply knowing that you have already won, even though you have nothing in your hands to prove it. It is a deep, inner confidence that assures you that by God's help, you are already victorious. Hebrews 11:1 says faith is now the substance of things you hope for and the evidence of things you do not yet have.

"Now faith is the substance of things hoped for, the evidence of things not seen." Hebrews 11:1 KJV

DREAMS, VISIONS, AND DESTINY

WINNING BY DREAMS

Whether we know it or not, we all have dreams, and at certain seasons in our spiritual development, we may even see visions. Dreams can be divided into two basic categories: spiritual dreams and life dreams. A spiritual dream is a seed from the invisible realm that typically appears during your sleep or rest. The ability to dream is a gift from God and often brings some form of understanding or interpretation to your life.

On the other hand, it is often the life dream that can be perceived as your big goals and the aspirations you desire to achieve. These may be based on your desires or passions and must be worked toward.

WINNING BY HAVING VISION

"Where there is no vision, the people perish..."
Proverbs 29:18-19 KJV

There are two main types of vision: spiritual and natural.

SPIRITUAL VISION: A spiritual vision comes from the Spirit of God. It can come while you are asleep, awake, or conscious. It appears as glimpses of a movie scene. Though you can be asleep or awake while seeing a vision, one thing that is certain about a vision is that you know for a fact that you saw what you saw and understood it very well. You are captivated by it, and it requires little to no interpretation.

THE NATURAL VISION: There is a vision you see in your conscious mind that may "pop up" as an idea or a thought. These ideas reflect what you would like to accomplish. In Joel 2, we are told that we shall dream dreams and see visions. Dreams are snapshots of your future and may sometimes be God's way of showing you how success is meant to manifest in your life.

The dream where you see yourself winning should be celebrated and fortified by prayer. The dream where you see yourself failing should be canceled and declared void, because you possess the spiritual power to shift that dream of failure into a dream of success by engaging the prayer of Prophetic Reversal. This prayer changes the outcome of bad dreams by altering their trajectory. **(See more in my book Power to Dream Again.)**

PLANNING FOR SUCCESS

WRITE THE VISION

Vision is greater than sight. In other words, you must see your success in the Invisible before you can see it in the Natural. Vision is what you see before it happens. It is a glimpse of your future or what is coming. In addition, your vision speaks to your goals, dreams, and ideas.

"1 I will stand upon my watch, and set me upon the tower, and will watch to see what he will say unto me, and what I shall answer when I am reproved. 2 And the Lord answered me, and said, Write the vision, and make it plain upon tables, that he may run that readeth it. 3 For the vision is yet for an appointed time, but at the end it shall speak, and not lie: though it tarry, wait for it; because it will surely come, it will not tarry."
Habakkuk 2:1-3 KJV

CREATE A VISION BOARD: Creating a vision board can serve as a guide to your future success. If you fail to plan, you have already planned to fail. In other words, you should put your goals on paper. Use pictures and images to help you see where you are going.

CREATE A BUSINESS PLAN: If you plan to start a business in the future, you must write a business plan. You must include the aim, objectives, demographics, financial budget, marketing plans, and more.

WRITE PLANS FOR YOUR MARRIAGE: You should never rush into marriage without seeking God. Marriage is not just a personal decision but a divine assignment. Therefore, you must ask for God's will to be done regarding your marriage, its timing, and the person you are to join your life with. You should create a *Marriage Spiritual Timetable* through prayer and discernment of God's will. This timetable helps you stay aligned with God's purpose for your life and can include the type of person you are called to marry, character and values, age range, cultural or ethnic considerations, and spiritual maturity.

Your timetable should also include **purpose**, that is, the reason for the union, along with plans for family, children, and legacy. No marriage can succeed unless it is planned for. Many people plan for a wedding more than for a marriage. This results in a successful wedding but an epic failure in marriage. A wedding lasts only a day, while a marriage requires a lifetime of intention, preparation, and communication. Success in marriage is not accidental; it comes only through strategic, intentional planning.

SPIRIT- LED INTELLIGENCE: THE WORD OF KNOWLEDGE AND DISCERNMENT

Winning by spiritual intelligence, particularly through the gifts of the word of knowledge and discernment, is crucial. As described in the Bible, these gifts enable believers to navigate life's complexities and fulfill God's purposes with divine insight and clarity. By seeking and developing these gifts, believers can fulfill God's purposes and experience victory in their spiritual journey. Let us, therefore, earnestly desire and cultivate spiritual intelligence, knowing that through it we can truly win in our walk with God.

"For to one is given by the Spirit the word of wisdom; to another the word of knowledge by the same Spirit."
1 Corinthians 12:8 KJV

Spiritual intelligence comes from the Holy Spirit. The verse above highlights that the gift of knowledge is from the Holy Spirit, equipping believers with divine understanding beyond human capacity. The Holy Spirit is the source of all spiritual gifts, including knowledge and discernment.

The word of knowledge serves a vital purpose in a believer's life. It provides supernatural insight into situations that would otherwise remain hidden. In John 16:13, Jesus says, "*Howbeit when he, the Spirit of truth, is come, he will guide you into all truth: for he shall not speak of himself; but whatsoever he shall hear, that shall he speak: and he will shew you things to come*." This passage emphasizes that the Holy Spirit reveals truth and future events, enabling believers to act with wisdom and foresight.

"But strong meat belongeth to them that are of full age, even those who by reason of use have their senses exercised to discern both good and evil." Hebrews 5:14 KJV

Discernment is another critical aspect of spiritual intelligence. The verse above underscores that mature believers develop discernment through practice and spiritual maturity. Discernment enables believers to distinguish between truth and deception, and between good and evil, guiding them to make righteous decisions.

Discernment protects against spiritual deception and danger. In 1 John 4:1, we are cautioned, "*Beloved, believe not every spirit, but try the spirits whether they are of God: because many false prophets are gone out into the world*." This instruction underscores the need for discernment to identify false teachings and influences, thereby safeguarding the believer's faith and integrity.

The word of knowledge directs us in our daily lives and ministries. Acts 5:3-4 offers an example: *"But Peter said, Ananias, why hath Satan filled thine heart to lie to the Holy Ghost, and to keep back part of the price of the land? Whiles it remained, was it not thine own? And after it was sold, was it not in thine own power? why hast thou conceived this thing in thine heart? thou hast not lied unto men, but unto God."* Here, Peter, through the word of knowledge, uncovers the deceit of Ananias, demonstrating how this gift can reveal hidden truths and bring correction.

Spiritual gifts, including the word of knowledge and discernment, are enduring and vital for the Church. In 1 Corinthians 13:8-10, we are told, *"Charity never faileth: but whether there be prophecies, they shall fail; whether there be tongues, they shall cease; whether there be knowledge, it shall vanish away. For we know in part, and we prophesy in part. But when that which is perfect is come, then that which is in part shall be done away."* This passage suggests that spiritual gifts are necessary until the fulfillment of God's kingdom, reinforcing their importance in the present age.

To walk in spiritual intelligence, believers must seek and cultivate these gifts through prayer and obedience to God's Word. James 1:5 encourages us, *"If any of you lack wisdom, let him ask of God, that giveth to all men liberally, and upbraideth not; and it shall be given him."* This verse assures believers that God generously grants wisdom to those who ask, empowering us with spiritual intelligence.

PLANNING FOR SUCCESS

SPIRITUAL MAGNETISM

Everything you do should be based on what God speaks, especially during certain seasons of your life. 1 Peter 5:8 states that the devil roams the earth as a roaring lion, seeking whom he may devour. Thus, if your attention, focus, and priorities are not centered on Christ, you will find that your time, energy, and resources are stolen by the enemy. The enemy despises the very idea of a Christian achieving success and therefore, Satan uses many tactics to ultimately destroy the believer.

You must begin to pursue your divine calling and purpose in God. Divine means God-ordained and God-orchestrated, and the act of pursuing implies adamantly going after something until it is achieved. Your purpose, that is, the original intent for which you were created, should be earnestly sought, as this purpose is what truly allows us to live a victorious life.

You must discover your calling in the Kingdom of God, where gifts are cultivated. Furthermore, these gifts must be cultivated through the formation of Godly relationships. Once these gifts have been cultivated, they will make room for you.

"A man's gift maketh room for him, and bringeth him before great men." Proverbs 18:16 KJV

When seeking to achieve any level of success, you must build relationships with those walking in greatness. You should connect only with others who can help deliver you and push you to discover your true purpose. Nonetheless, it is important to note that those who are not part of your destiny are automatically part of your history, as these individuals are in no way contributing to or investing in your future.

Further, you must begin to analyze the relationships you find yourself in, whether they involve family, friends, or others like them. The worst relationship to be in is a parasitic one. In this type of relationship, a person comes alongside you simply for the benefits. This relationship is one-sided, draining, and only benefits the second party involved while harming and eventually destroying you. If someone is not pushing you toward your purpose, to your destiny, and through open doors, they are pushing you away from your purpose and should not be permitted to remain in your life. On the other hand, the best relationship is a symbiotic one. In this relationship, both parties contribute to success and therefore share in the victory. In a symbiotic relationship, trust is evident, and when one person achieves favor, victory, or success, both parties succeed.

WISDOM OF A SOUND RELATIONSHIP

Many people remain trapped in cycles of lack and limitation because they have not learned to properly recognize, honor, and maximize the relationships God has already placed around them. If you enter relationships only to receive, you will never gain access to the deeper dimensions of wealth.

True wealth is not limited to money. In fact, one of the greatest forms of wealth is the relationship itself. The ability to access wisdom, counsel, direction, correction, opportunity, and support from others is a form of prosperity that many overlook. Sometimes the greatest value in a relationship is not financial but may be insight, guidance, influence, or even encouragement that shapes your destiny.

God often gives ideas and, with them, divine connections. Yet many people miss these connections because they see relationships only through the lens of personal gain rather than purpose and assignment. You should not pursue relationships merely because you expect to need something from someone later. Instead, you should pursue relationships to learn, to serve, and to grow. This is the wisdom of sound relationships.

God strategically aligns your life with people and opportunities for growth. Joseph is a powerful example of this principle. Before he stepped into leadership, he faithfully served his father. Later, he served in Potiphar's house with excellence, and eventually served within Pharaoh's sphere of influence. At every stage, service was the pathway to elevation. One dream positioned him, but consistent service prepared him.

The Bible teaches that your gift is designed to make room for you and to bring you before kings and great men. Therefore, it is essential that you discover who these "kings and great men" are. It is important to note that not every relationship is transactional, and not every connection is meant for financial exchange. In fact, many of the most valuable relationships are built on wisdom, trust, character, and shared purpose.

You should always enter relationships with authenticity in mind: with sincerity, not manipulation. You should enter into relationships to serve, learn, add value, and build, as this ultimately ensures wealth and success. Trust is one of the most powerful currencies in any relationship. When people trust you, they open doors for you; however, when trust is broken or absent, relationships go nowhere. The story of Ruth and Naomi beautifully illustrates this. Orpah chose to leave because she evaluated the relationship in terms of what she could gain. When there was no visible benefit, she departed. However, Ruth chose covenant over convenience. She remained committed even when there was nothing material to gain. Through her loyalty, service, and devotion, Ruth transitioned from obscurity to destiny. Naomi had nothing material to offer her, yet she gave her something far greater, including a relationship, wisdom, and spiritual covering. This connection ultimately positioned Ruth for one of the most significant destinies in Scripture.

To truly become successful, you must first learn to function on every level of life: spiritually, mentally, emotionally, financially, and relationally. Once you are able to do this, you have begun to master the hallmark of true success. One of the foundational truths of success is learning to relate to, connect with, and effectively engage with people from all walks of life. You must learn to treasure relationships, recognizing their value beyond surface-level interaction. Every relationship offers an opportunity to learn, grow, and gain insight. When properly understood, relationships become one of life's greatest assets.

On the road to success, I have come to learn that several key elements are required. These are what I call the 3 H's of success, and they are as follows:

- **Holiness:** The state of being morally pure, spiritually whole, and dedicated to a sacred purpose.

- **Humility:** Having a modest view of one's own importance and being free from excessive pride and arrogance.

- **Honesty:** Possessing the moral virtue of being truthful, authentic, and free from deceit in words, actions, or deeds.

PLANNING FOR SUCCESS

THE LAW OF ATTRACTION

The Law of Attraction refers to a moral principle which states that like attracts like; that the thoughts, beliefs, and emotions, a person consistently projects outward will draw corresponding people, circumstances, and outcomes into their life. It is built upon the understanding that human beings are not passive recipients of life's events, but active participants in shaping their realities through the orientation of their Spiritual Inner Man engineered by the power of the Holy Spirit. At its most foundational level, the Law of Attraction asserts three primary truths:

- Your dominant spirit led thoughts and feelings create an invisible "frequency" that the world responds to.
- Positive, expectant, grateful thinking draws favorable outcomes, relationships, and open doors.
- Negative, fearful, or doubtful thinking reinforces and multiplies unfavorable conditions.

Kingdom relationships are divinely appointed by God and are usually formed to advance the purpose of the Kingdom. These relationships usually provide equal blessings to all involved and generally point you toward your spiritual destiny.

ATTRACTION IN GODLY RELATIONSHIPS

There are many principles that govern the concept of attraction in Godly relationships. Some of these principles include but are not limited to:

Principle 1: You Attract Who You Are, Not Just Who You Want: One of the most important relational truths embedded in the Law of Attraction is this: you attract at the level of who you are, not merely at the level of what you desire. A person who has not done the internal work of healing, wholeness, and identity will continue to attract relationships that mirror their unresolved wounds and beliefs.("Can two walk together, except they be agreed?" Amos 3:3)

Principle 2: What You Focus On In Relationships Grows
The Law of Attraction teaches that whatever receives your sustained attention, whether desired or feared, expands in your experience. This is profoundly true in covenant relationships: marriage, family, friendship, and ministry partnerships.

Principle 3: Clarity of Desire Produces Clarity of Result
Vague desires attract vague outcomes. The person who prays generally, "Lord, send me someone nice", will often find their relational life similarly vague and undefined. Kingdom attraction requires specificity of vision and intentionality of prayer. ("Write the vision, and make it plain upon tables, that he may run that readeth it." Habakkuk 2:2)

Principle 4: You Must Become an Environment for What You Are Attracting: Kingdom relationships do not appear in a vacuum. God places people in environments where covenant connections are possible. The believer who isolates, withholds, and refuses to serve others creates a relational climate of lack. The believer who is generous, open, faithful, and actively present in community creates fertile ground for deep, lasting relationships. This includes actions such as:

▪ Serving in your local church: kingdom connections are found in the house of God.

- Operating with integrity in business: people of character attract people of character.

- Cultivating thankfulness: a grateful spirit is magnetically attractive to others.

- Healing your inner wounds: unhealed trauma repels the very relationships you desire.

SPIRITUAL MUTUALISM

Each person involved in a Godly, Mutualistic Relationship can give as well as receive. There is no manipulation, condemnation, or control. This relationship does not take you out of the will of God; on the contrary, it leads you toward fulfilling the purpose and plan of God. Several people demonstrated this type of Godly relationship. For example, Naomi and Ruth, David and Jonathan, and Elijah and Elisha.

- **Ruth and Naomi** had more than a mother-in-law/daughter-in-law relationship. Ruth was deeply devoted to Naomi, even when she had nothing to offer. Ruth declared: ***"entreat me not to leave thee ... for whither thou goest I will go and where thou lodgest, I will lodge. Thy people shall be my people and thy God, my God ..." Ruth 1:16-17 KJV***

- **David and Jonathan** also shared a kindred spirit marked by deep loyalty and respect. Jonathan was willing to protect David at all costs, even against his father, King Saul. According to 1 Samuel 20:17, this covenant was rooted in love.

"... for he loved him as he loved his own soul."
1 Samuel 20:17 KJV

- Furthermore, **Elisha and Elijah** exemplified a Godly soul tie. In 1 Kings 19, Elisha desired to follow and serve Elijah, the man of God. He sacrificed his inheritance, poured water on Elijah's hands, and declared with his own mouth that he would not break rank or look back, because he realized that "looking back is death." As a result of his loyalty, Elisha received Elijah's mantle and a double portion of his anointing.

"...Here is Elisha the son of Shaphat, which poured water on the hands of Elijah." 2 Kings 3:11 KJV

Godly soul ties are designed to help you become the person God intended you to be. We all need "Naomis" in our lives, spiritual mothers who help birth us into our divine destiny. We all need "Jonathans" who are willing to sacrifice for us, even at the expense of denying ourselves, our privileges, and our prestige. Finally, we all need "Elijahs" who are willing to mentor and mold us so that we are equipped to fulfill our God-ordained purposes.

THE LAW OF ATTRACTION IN KINGDOM BUSINESS

Business is a Kingdom tool. The marketplace is one of the seven mountains of cultural influence, and God has called His people to occupy it with excellence, integrity, and Kingdom values. When applied properly in business, the Law of Attraction is simply Kingdom Stewardship: positioning yourself, your brand, your company, and your culture to attract clients, partnerships, capital, and opportunities that align with your God-given assignment.

"Seest thou a man diligent in his business? He shall stand before kings; he shall not stand before mean men." Proverbs 22:29 KJV

How the Law of Attraction Operates in Business

Although often overlooked, the law of attraction is extremely prevalent in the business arena and is governed by various protocols, including:

A. *Your Brand Reflects Your Internal Belief System:* A business owner who does not believe in the value of their product or service will unconsciously communicate that doubt through pricing, presentation, and persistence. Confidence and conviction are attractive. Doubt and apology are repellent. Kingdom business begins with the understanding that your assignment has God-ordained value, and you must carry it out accordingly.

B. *Culture Attracts Clients and Partners:* Businesses grounded in integrity, excellence, generosity, and genuine service cultivate a culture that draws loyal customers and strategic partners. Your business environment, whether physical or digital, signals what you believe about yourself and your clients. Invest in it. Steward it with excellence.

C. *Your Network is Your Net Worth:* This well-known business principle is rooted in biblical truth. The connections God sends you are not random; they are covenantal and strategic. Treat every business relationship as a divine assignment. The person you serve faithfully today may open a door tomorrow that no one else can.

"A man's gift maketh room for him, and bringeth him before great men." Proverbs 18:16 KJV

D. *Sowing & Reaping:* Every seed sown in business, whether a generous act, a quality product, an honest transaction, or a prayer of blessing over a client, yields a harvest. The Law of Attraction in Kingdom business is ultimately the Law of Sowing and Reaping, applied with faith, strategy, and excellence.

Whatever you sow, you shall eventually reap. For instance:

- Sow excellence; attract excellent clients.
- Sow integrity; attract trustworthy partnerships.
- Sow generosity; attract supernatural provision.
- Sow prayer; attract divine favor and open doors.

"Be not deceived; God is not mocked: for whatsoever a man soweth, that shall he also reap." Galatians 6:7 KJV

The Law of Attraction is real because God designed it. However, in its purest, most powerful form, it is not the law of the universe responding to some human vibration. It is the law of covenant responding to faith. It is the law of sowing responding to reaping. It is the law of wisdom responding to diligence. It is the principle of declaration responding to the word of God.

When we, as believers, understand the Law of Attraction through a Kingdom lens, we become one of the most powerful forces in any room, attracting godly relationships, unprecedented success, and divine business alignment, not by might nor by power, but by the Spirit of God working through a yielded, faith-filled, diligent, and aligned life.

"Delight thyself also in the LORD; and he shall give thee the desires of thine heart." Psalm 37:4 KJV

DESTINED TO WIN

"For we are his workmanship, created in Christ Jesus unto good works, which God hath before ordained that we should walk in them." Ephesians 2:10 KJV

CHAPTER EIGHT

UNDERSTANDING GIFTS, TALENTS, AND ABILITIES

What is the difference between spiritual gifts and natural talents? Natural talents are physical abilities to do special things. These abilities may be developed through practice, or they may be innate, coming naturally and requiring little to no effort. Some natural talents may include musical ability, carpentry, cooking, mechanical aptitude, and artistic skills, among others.

On the other hand, spiritual gifts are spiritual endowments given by the Holy Spirit to accomplish something for the Kingdom of God. The major difference between a natural talent or ability and a spiritual gift is the anointing of God. The Greek term for a spiritual gift is **charismata:** χάρισμα (singular) or χαρίσματα (plural). The English word "charisma" originates from this word.

In 1 Corinthians 12, two Greek terms are translated as "spiritual gifts," referring to enablement or extraordinary capabilities that God has bestowed upon an individual to advance God's Kingdom. Because these gifts are freely given by God, they cannot be corrupted by carnal influences or used to satisfy human desires. Instead, spiritual gifts are given to the Body of Christ to ultimately bring glory to God.

In Christianity, a *charism* is an endowment or extraordinary power given by the Holy Spirit. Spiritual charisma draws individuals to the person endowed with such power; however, it is up to that person to direct them to God and the things of God. These are supernatural graces given to individual Christians to fulfill the church's mission.

Natural talents often serve as the means by which spiritual gifts are expressed. For example, a Christian vocalist may have the spiritual gift of evangelism expressed through their musical talent. Regardless of natural talent or spiritual gift, only the anointing of God will truly make a difference.

CORE PERSONALITY TRAITS

Four basic personality or character traits are said to define an individual. Your personality helps to "paint" the canvas of your life. It serves as a complement or catalyst to your spiritual gift and can be cultivated or enhanced to facilitate the work of the ministry. It is important to note that some people may demonstrate most of the characteristics of one trait (called the dominant trait) and fewer of another (called the subdominant trait). These traits are considered inherent and have been passed down through generations. These personality frameworks are:

TYPE A: The (Work-Oriented) Choleric – These are people who are serious-minded and goal-oriented. They are succinct in their communication and highly focused.

Some of the character strengths and weaknesses associated with this personality trait include:

Strengths:	**Weaknesses:**
Efficient	Rigid & Unbendable
Plans well	Domineering
Resolute/decisive	Intolerant & Impatient
Independent Thinker	Anxious
Self-motivator	Insensitivity

TYPE B: The (People-Oriented) Sanguine – These people are usually easy-going, people-pleasers. They are very friendly and will promise you "the world" and, if they could, would do everything within their natural ability to make it happen.

Some of the character strengths and weaknesses of people with this personality trait are:

Strengths:	**Weaknesses:**
Friendly/Easy going	Easily persuaded
Passionate	Disorganized
Sociable	Undisciplined
Creative	Short attention span
Compassionate	Easily Distracted

TYPE C: The (Analytical-Perfectionist Melancholy) – These individuals are highly organized and detail-oriented. They carefully analyze situations and have a remarkable ability to notice even the smallest details, much like finding a "needle in a haystack." They prefer tasks completed in a specific way and often expect others to follow the same standards. When things do not go as planned, they may react strongly and view the situation as far more serious than it is.

They cannot handle disappointments, failures, or shortcomings in themselves or others. They are serious-minded and thoughtful; however, they may struggle with depression, sadness, and pessimism. Without the regulation of the Holy Spirit, these persons can develop extreme obsessive-compulsive disorders, becoming overly consumed with their weight, appearance, cleanliness, inadequacies, personality flaws, and more.

Some of the character strengths and weaknesses of persons with this personality trait are:

Strengths:	**Weaknesses:**
Detailed Oriented	Chronically Depressed
Perfectionist	Easily Offended
Organized	Extremely Negative
Disciplined	Sensitive
Discerning	Insecure
	Self-centered & Critical

The (Easy-Going) Phlegmatic – These people appear to be unaffected by life's "goings on." They are very easy to get along with and do not allow themselves to be moved by situations, circumstances, or people. They are usually quiet and may even be considered passive.

Some of the character strengths and weaknesses of people with this personality trait are:

Strengths:	**Weaknesses:**
Humble	Unorganized
Easy-going	Skeptical
Peacemaker	Unmotivated
Flexible	Quiet/Passive
Avoids Confrontation	Procrastinator
	Overly Confidential

THE POWER OF NETWORKING: CASTING YOUR NET ON THE RIGHT SIDE

Networking, in a spiritual sense, is about building relationships and connecting with others in ways that fulfill God's purposes. The Bible offers many principles and examples showing how divine networking can lead to success and fulfillment within God's plan.

The concept of networking is illustrated in the Bible by Jesus' instruction to His disciples to cast their net on the right side. In John 21:6, we read, *"And he said unto them, Cast the net on the right side of the ship, and ye shall find. They cast therefore, and now they were not able to draw it for the multitude of fishes."* This miracle illustrates the importance of following divine guidance in our efforts, ensuring fruitful results. It signifies that success in our endeavors comes from heeding God's direction.

Obedience to God's instructions is crucial in networking. When the disciples followed Jesus' command, they experienced an overwhelming catch. Proverbs 3:5-6 advises, *"Trust in the LORD with all thine heart; and lean not unto thine own understanding. In all thy ways acknowledge him, and he shall direct thy paths."* This scripture emphasizes that trusting and acknowledging God in all our interactions and decisions leads to successful outcomes. By seeking His guidance, we align our efforts with His will, ensuring our networks are blessed and productive. Networking should be purposeful, aimed at advancing God's Kingdom and fulfilling His purposes on earth.

"Two are better than one; because they have a good reward for their labour. For if they fall, the one will lift up his fellow: but woe to him that is alone when he falleth; for he hath not another to help him up." Ecclesiastes 4:9-10 KJV

This passage highlights the strength and support found in Godly relationships. By building and nurturing meaningful connections, we can support and uplift each other, enhancing our collective strength and effectiveness. The early church exemplified the power of community and networking. Acts 2:44-47 describes their unity and shared purpose:

"44 And all that believed were together, and had all things common; 45 And sold their possessions and goods, and parted them to all men, as every man had need. 46 And they, continuing daily with one accord in the temple, and breaking bread from house to house, did eat their meat with gladness and singleness of heart, 47 Praising God, and having favour with all the people. And the Lord added to the church daily such as should be saved." Acts 2:44-47 KJV

This community's devotion to one another and to God's mission resulted in growth and favor. Their example shows how unity and shared purpose in networking can lead to both spiritual and numerical growth.

God orchestrates divine appointments that foster meaningful connections. Proverbs 16:9 affirms, *"A man's heart deviseth his way: but the LORD directeth his steps."* This verse reminds us that while we may plan our paths, God ultimately directs our steps. By being sensitive to His leading, we can recognize and seize opportunities to connect with the right people at the right time, leading to divinely ordained outcomes.

Networking should always be conducted with integrity and love. Colossians 3:23-24 advises, "And whatsoever ye do, do it heartily, as to the Lord, and not unto men; Knowing that of the Lord ye shall receive the reward of the inheritance: for ye serve the Lord Christ." This scripture encourages believers to approach their interactions and relationships with sincerity and excellence, knowing that their ultimate service is to the Lord. Integrity in networking builds trust and reflects the character of Christ.

GOAL SETTING

"Commit thy works unto the Lord, and thy thoughts shall be established." Proverbs 16:3 KJV

What is a goal? A goal is an aim, objective, or desire that a person seeks to achieve. It is something great that you believe God will accomplish. Goals can be personal, professional, short-term, long-term, or even spiritual.

Personal Goal – Personal goals are objectives and aims that a person seeks to achieve in various aspects of their life. These goals can involve striving towards something, maintaining a certain state, or avoiding it entirely. For instance, a personal goal might be to reduce weekly fast-food intake or reach a specific body weight within a set timeframe.

Professional Goal – Professional goals are objectives and aims that a person seeks to achieve in their career and work life. These may include aiming for a specific position in the workplace, targeting a desired salary, or securing a job at a preferred company.

Long-Term Goal – Long-term goals are objectives and aims a person seeks to achieve over an extended period. These goals require careful planning and preparation as they are not expected to be achieved in the near future. Although they may take years to achieve, the actions and decisions made in the present play a crucial role in determining whether these goals will ultimately be successful. An example of a long-term goal may involve purchasing your dream house or dream car, as it is not expected to be achieved within the upcoming week or month but requires commitment and planning.

Short-Term Goal – Short-term goals are objectives set to be achieved in the near future. These goals are typically expected to be achieved within a year and require strategic planning and effective preparation, given their short timeline. For instance, a person may set out to read three books in a month. This is considered a short-term goal because it can be accomplished within that timeframe.

Spiritual Goal – Spiritual goals are objectives and aims set to be achieved within an individual's spiritual life. These goals are centered on Christ and arise from a person's desire to grow in their faith and relationship with God. An example of a spiritual goal may involve a person setting out to spend more time in prayer, worship, or fasting unto God.

Goal setting should not be done simply because it looks good or as an aesthetic. However, goal setting should be driven by a genuine desire and passion to achieve a specific aim. Setting goals is an essential aspect of a person's growth, development, and maturity, and provides not only a sense of direction but also motivation, drive, and focus on what should truly be prioritized and worked toward. Goals, whether short-term or long-term, serve as a roadmap for guidance and direction for individuals on their journey toward growth, self-development, and success, and should be utilized by every individual with a true and keen desire to achieve victory in life.

Setting goals gives us clarity, direction, and purpose. When we define our goals, whether to develop a closer relationship with Christ, attend church more frequently, improve a skill, advance in a career, or achieve personal milestones, we create a clear path forward. Outlining a goal also helps us gain insight into what we should be working toward, providing guidance and direction. This clarity helps us make decisions and take actions that align with our objectives, reducing distractions and unnecessary detours. In the absence of a goal, loss is bound to occur because there is nothing to work toward. While a victory may occur, it may also be short-lived, as it was never a clearly outlined goal.

In addition, goals provide motivation and drive. A clearly outlined goal gives us something to strive for and inspires us to work harder, smarter, and more strategically to ensure that our goals are accomplished. Without goals, it is easy to feel lost or aimless, lacking the motivation to make progress or even to work toward a task. When we set specific, achievable, and realistic goals, we create a sense of urgency and commitment to our own growth and development. When those goals are not met, it shows that we either didn't plan efficiently, didn't allocate our time wisely, or didn't take important factors into account.

While the failure to achieve a goal may feel discouraging in the present moment, it allows us to adjust our approach so that success is more likely in the future. Conversely, when no goal has been established, failure offers no clear direction for adjustment or growth. As a result, individuals often find themselves repeating the same mistakes and remaining trapped in cycles of failure.

Moreover, goals foster accountability, responsibility, and liability. Because there is no one else to blame for the achievement or failure of the goals we set, we take ownership of our actions and outcomes. Because of this increased accountability, we take our tasks seriously and find ways to achieve our goals, come what may.

We become more proactive in managing and allocating our time and resources effectively, recognizing that the effort we put in directly impacts our ability to achieve those goals and is a candid reflection of who we are. Being held accountable through goal setting promotes self-discipline and helps us push through life's difficult obstacles as we learn to overcome challenges and setbacks along the way.

Setting goals also promotes personal growth and self-development. When we set goals, we are pushed out of our comfort zones, as we are required to take ambitious actions to ultimately achieve our desired objectives. For example, a person may be required to attend an event they typically wouldn't or learn a new skill they normally wouldn't, simply to achieve a goal.

Whether we succeed or fail, the process of achieving our goals teaches us lifelong lessons and helps us grow as individuals. It helps us learn from our mistakes, gain valuable lessons, and develop a winning mindset, all of which are critical in today's spiritual realm and fast-paced world.

PLANNING FOR SUCCESS

When setting goals, individuals often fail to achieve what they set out to do because their goals lack a timeline or are highly unrealistic. Setting a timeline for a goal is extremely important and plays a major role in achieving it. An outlined timeline not only allows us to measure progress but also helps limit procrastination and fosters motivation, as it is simply human nature to be driven to meet a deadline. On the contrary, if a timeline is not set for a goal, it allows for much procrastination, as there is no need to push or drive to meet a deadline.

As previously stated, a spiritual goal centers on a genuine desire to build a closer relationship with God. As believers, though we may aspire to achieve success, our top priority should be spiritual. It is simply a waste of time to set a spiritual goal and then spend no time working toward it. Your spiritual aptitude refers to your level of spirituality and the time you spend cultivating a relationship with God. Your spiritual aptitude includes:

- The amount of time spent with God
- The number of hours spent reading the Bible
- Time spent in prayer
- Time spent in worship
- Church attendance
- Volunteer record in faith-based activities and initiatives. For instance, my husband and I are supporters of *Camp Believe.*
- Evangelizing/Witnessing
- Fasting/ Consecration

LIVING LIFE AT THE MASTERY LEVEL

It is a proven fact that God performs miracles. Without a shadow of a doubt, God creates signs and wonders that show and reveal His matchless power. However, true success is not merely living on the edge of happenstance or miracles; it is learning to live in a state of mastery. Miracles reveal God's power, but mastery reveals growth, discipline, wisdom, stewardship, and maturity. A successful person should not only need rescue; they should become equipped to rule, govern, build, manage, and sustain what God has placed in their hands. But what exactly is "mastery"?

Mastery is the highest level of developed skill, knowledge, wisdom, and competence in a particular area of life. It is the ability to consistently produce desired results because you have learned, practiced, understood, and disciplined yourself in that area. It is the state of having comprehensive knowledge, exceptional skill, and self-control that enables a person to perform effectively, consistently, and confidently. Mastery is not perfection. It is the continual pursuit of excellence through learning, experience, discipline, and application.

Biblical Perspective of Mastery

In Scripture, mastery is often connected to diligence, wisdom, stewardship, discipline, and maturity.

"Seest thou a man diligent in his business? he shall stand before kings; he shall not stand before mean men." Proverbs 22:29 KJV

"And every man that striveth for the mastery is temperate in all things." 1 Corinthians 9:25 KJV

PLANNING FOR SUCCESS

Mastery is demonstrated throughout Scripture by men and women who developed exceptional wisdom, skill, discipline, leadership, stewardship, and faithfulness in their God-given assignments.

- *Joseph: Mastery of Administration and Stewardship*: Joseph mastered leadership, economics, planning, and resource management. He went from prisoner to prime minister because he demonstrated extraordinary competence and wisdom. ***("And Pharaoh said unto Joseph, Forasmuch as God hath shewed thee all this, there is none so discreet and wise as thou art: Thou shalt be over my house, and according unto thy word shall all my people be ruled..." Genesis 41:39-40 KJV)***

- *Daniel - Mastery of Knowledge and Excellence*: Daniel became one of the most influential men in Babylon because of his wisdom, discipline, and excellent spirit. ***("Then this Daniel was preferred above the presidents and princes, because an excellent spirit was in him..." Daniel 6:3 KJV)***

- *Solomon - Mastery of Wisdom*: Solomon is perhaps the greatest biblical example of mastery through wisdom. ***("And God gave Solomon wisdom and understanding exceeding much..." 1 Kings 4:29-30 KJV)***

- *David - Mastery of Warfare and Worship*: Before David became king, he mastered his sling, his worship, and his relationship with God. David's victory over Goliath was not luck; it was the result of years of preparation. ***("And he took his staff in his hand, and chose him five smooth stones..." 1 Samuel 17:40 KJV)***

- *Bezalel - Mastery of Craftsmanship:* God specifically anointed Bezalel with wisdom and skill to build the Tabernacle. ***("And I have filled him with the spirit of God, in wisdom, and in understanding, and in knowledge, and in all manner of workmanship." Exodus 31:3-5 KJV)***

- *Paul - Mastery of Ministry and Doctrine*: Paul became one of the greatest apostles because of his disciplined life, theological understanding, and commitment to God's calling. ***("And every man that striveth for the mastery is temperate in all things." 1 Corinthians 9:25 KJV)***

- *Nehemiah - Mastery of Vision and Project Management:* Nehemiah successfully rebuilt Jerusalem's walls despite opposition and limited resources.

- *Moses - Mastery of Leadership*: Moses led millions of people through the wilderness for forty years.

- *The Proverbs 31 Woman* - Mastery of Life Management: The virtuous woman demonstrates mastery in multiple areas of life simultaneously. '

- *Jesus Christ - The Ultimate Example of Mastery*: Jesus is the perfect example of mastery because He mastered every assignment given to Him by the Father. Jesus knew when to pray, when to preach, when to heal, when to rest, when to confront, and when to remain silent. ***("I have glorified thee on the earth: I have finished the work which thou gavest me to do." John 17:4 KJV)***

The Elite Mastery Structure: E.L.I.T.E.

Those who achieve mastery understand that lasting success is built on key principles that shape character, influence, and performance. These principles include:

E: *Excellence in everything you do*

L: *Lifelong learning and development*

I: *Integrity and character*

T: *Time stewardship and disciplined habits*

E: *Empowering others through mentorship and legacy*

THE MARK OF MASTER BUILDERS

The following are some of the characteristics of mastery:

1. Knowledge: Knowing what to do.
2. Wisdom: Knowing when to do it.
3. Skill: Knowing how to do it.
4. Discipline: Doing it consistently.
5. Experience: Learning through practice.
6. Stewardship: Managing resources effectively.
7. Self-Control: Governing yourself before governing others.
8. Excellence: Continually improving.
9. Attention to Details: Learning to take note of and pay attention to seemingly small or minute details, looking at information that may seem or appear insignificant.

Attention to detail is the ability to recognize, manage, and perfect the small things that others often overlook. Masters understand that greatness is often hidden in details and a master knows that details determine quality, credibility, and results.

10. Measurement: Taking stock of volume or how much you have. Measurement Masters measure what matters. They track progress, evaluate results, identify weaknesses, and make adjustments.

11. Capacity: Knowing your limitations. What are you able to carry. Capacity is the ability to handle greater levels of responsibility, pressure, resources, opportunities, influence, and success.

Capacity includes:

- Spiritual Capacity
- Mental Capacity
- Emotional Capacity
- Leadership Capacity
- Financial Capacity
- Relational Capacity

12. Time Management: Understanding the value of time and using it wisely, productively, and intentionally. Masters do not merely spend time; they invest it. They prioritize what is important, eliminate distractions, maximize opportunities, and organize their lives around purpose. Time is one of God's greatest gifts, and those who master their time often master their lives.

ANOINTING AND UNCTION TO WIN

"...Not by might, nor by power, but by my spirit, saith the LORD of hosts." Zechariah 4:6 KJV

Winning by unction, or the anointing, is essential. This involves living under the Holy Spirit's divine empowerment and guidance, and it is through this anointing that believers receive wisdom, power, protection, and the ability to fulfill God's purposes. As we embrace the anointing, we are equipped to navigate life's challenges victoriously and advance God's kingdom on earth. Therefore, we must continually seek and cherish the anointing, knowing that it is through this divine unction that we truly win.

The anointing originates from God. In 1 John 2:20, we read, *"But ye have an unction from the Holy One, and ye know all things."* This verse underscores that the anointing is a divine endowment from the Holy Spirit, equipping believers with wisdom and discernment. The Holy Spirit is the agent of this anointing, and His presence in our lives is a mark of God's favor and empowerment.

The Holy Spirit provides believers with divine wisdom, enabling them to understand God's will and make decisions that align with His purposes. This wisdom surpasses human understanding and allows believers to navigate complex life situations with clarity and insight. The anointing imparts supernatural power to believers. This power is evident in various ways, such as the ability to perform miracles, heal the sick, and proclaim the gospel with boldness and effectiveness. It's a manifestation of God's presence working through individuals to accomplish what is humanly impossible.

The Holy Spirit also offers protection to believers, serving as a safeguard against spiritual attacks and deception. It ensures that believers remain steadfast in their faith and are not led astray by false teachings or worldly temptations. The anointing equips believers to fulfill the specific callings and missions God has for them, ranging from ministering in their local communities to serving as missionaries in distant lands. The Holy Spirit guides and empowers them to accomplish these tasks effectively.

The anointing is upon you to win. God has placed His divine grace, power, favor, wisdom, and authority upon your life so that you can overcome every obstacle, defeat every attack of the enemy, and fulfill your God-given purpose. The anointing empowers you to rise above fear, discouragement, limitation, and failure. It can shift the very trajectory of your life, especially when you are connected to the right Spiritual Leaders. The anointing gives you strength in difficult seasons, clarity in moments of confusion, and courage to move forward even when the odds are stacked high against you.

You are not fighting in your own strength; heaven is backing you. Angelic assistance is at your disposal and all you have to do is engage this realm. The anointing breaks yokes, opens doors, releases supernatural favor, and positions you for victory in every area of your life. Through prayer, obedience, consecration, and intimacy with God, the anointing upon your life will continue to grow and produce fruit. No matter the battles you face, remember that God did not anoint you to lose; He anointed you for success, and He has anointed you to win.

YOU WILL WIN

Winning is in your DNA, so there is no denying it. Therefore, one truth must remain anchored in your spirit: you will win. No matter what opposition you have faced, no matter the warfare, setbacks, disappointments, betrayals, delays, or struggles, your story does not end in defeat. God did not create you to fail. He created you with purpose, power, destiny, and divine potential. The same God who called you is the same God who will sustain you, strengthen you, and establish you. Your victory has already been written in heaven.

There will be seasons in your life when it feels as though the pressure is too heavy and the battle is too intense. There will be moments when doors close unexpectedly, people walk away, resources become limited, and circumstances seem uncertain. Yet even in those moments, you must remember that God never abandons His people. Every challenge you face is developing strength, wisdom, endurance, and spiritual maturity within you. The trials were never sent to destroy you; they were sent to prepare you. Through every test, God has been positioning you for greater levels of success and purpose.

You will win because you are not fighting your battles alone. Heaven is backing you. The power of God is working on your behalf even when you cannot see it. Angels are being dispatched on your behalf. Divine favor is surrounding you. The Holy Spirit is leading you into truth, wisdom, and understanding. God has already equipped you with spiritual tools that empower you for victory in every area of your life.

You will win through the gifts of the Spirit. The Holy Spirit has given believers supernatural abilities to overcome obstacles, discern danger, operate in wisdom, and walk in divine authority. The gifts of wisdom, discernment, faith, prophecy, healing, and knowledge are not just spiritual experiences; they are weapons for victorious living. When you operate in the Spirit, you gain access to divine strategies that natural understanding cannot provide. God will give you wisdom for your family, direction for your ministry, solutions for your career, and insight concerning your future. The Spirit of God will guide you into success.

You will win through the power of intercessory prayer. Prayer changes atmospheres, shifts circumstances, and releases heaven's intervention into earthly situations. There is power in persistent prayer. Every time you pray, chains are broken, strongholds are weakened, and doors begin to open. Prayer strengthens your inner man and aligns you with the will of God. Through intercession, you can stand in the gap not only for yourself but also for your family, community, ministry, and generation. Never underestimate the power of a believer who knows how to pray. Your prayers are creating victories that you may not even see yet.

You will win when you find your place at the altar of consecration. Success without surrender can be dangerous, but success born of intimacy with God produces lasting fruit. The altar is where pride is broken, character is refined, and spiritual authority is developed. God uses the hidden place to prepare His people for public victories. Every moment spent in worship, obedience, sacrifice, and surrender strengthens your spiritual foundation. The altar produces endurance, humility, and maturity. When your life is built upon the altar, nothing the enemy sends against you can destroy you.

You will also win through seasons of fasting and prayer. Fasting sharpens your spiritual sensitivity and deepens your connection with God. It silences distractions, weakens the flesh, and empowers the spirit. There are breakthroughs that only come through prayer and fasting. Throughout Scripture, great victories were preceded by consecration. Fasting positions you to hear clearly from God and receive divine direction for your life. In times of uncertainty, fasting brings clarity. In times of weakness, it releases strength. In times of warfare, it activates spiritual authority. Your consecration is preparing you for victory.

You will win when you embrace the dreams and visions God has placed inside of you. God speaks through visions, dreams, prophetic revelation, and divine inspiration. The enemy often attacks vision because he knows that vision produces purpose and movement. Never allow disappointment, fear, or delay to make you abandon what God has shown you. The vision may take time, but it will surely come to pass. God has placed greatness within you, and every promise He has spoken concerning your life will manifest in its appointed season. Protect your vision. Pray over your dreams. Stay focused on your assignment. What God has ordained for you cannot be stopped.

You will win because you have access to the supernatural realm. As a believer, you are not limited to natural resources alone. Heaven responds to faith, obedience, and spiritual alignment. Throughout your journey, God will release supernatural help, divine connections, miraculous provision, protection, and unexpected opportunities. Angels are ministering spirits sent to assist those who belong to God. The supernatural power of God is real, active, and available. Even when you cannot trace His hand, God is still moving behind the scenes on your behalf.

Most importantly, you will win when you walk in Godly wisdom. Wisdom is the foundation of sustainable success. It teaches you when to act, when to wait, when to speak, and when to remain silent. It protects you from unnecessary battles and destructive decisions. When you seek God's wisdom, you gain understanding beyond human reasoning. Godly wisdom will guide your relationships, finances, ministry, career, and personal life. Heaven supports those who choose righteousness, integrity, humility, and obedience.

As you continue your journey, remember that success is not defined solely by material possessions or public recognition. True success is becoming all that God created you to be. It means fulfilling your purpose, walking in obedience, maintaining your faith, and impacting others for the Kingdom of God. Success is finding peace in the midst of storms, strength in adversity, and joy even through difficult seasons. Success is knowing that your life is aligned with the will of God.

There will be moments when you grow weary, but do not give up. There will be times when progress feels slow, but do not quit. The process may be painful, yet the promise remains alive. God is faithful to complete the work He started in you. Every prayer you have prayed, every sacrifice you have made, every tear you have shed, and every battle you have endured have not been in vain. Your labor will bear fruit. Your faithfulness will be rewarded.

Remember that you are equipped, empowered, and anointed for success in every dimension of your life. You are empowered to succeed spiritually, emotionally, mentally, financially, relationally, and professionally. God desires that you walk in wholeness, victory, and purpose. The principles in these pages are practical tools to help you grow stronger in prayer, sharper in discernment, deeper in faith, and more effective in fulfilling your divine assignment.

No matter where you are today, your future remains full of possibilities. God is not finished with you yet. Your greatest victories may still lie ahead. Continue to pray. Continue to fast. Continue to believe. Continue to trust God's timing. Continue to walk by faith, not by sight. As you move forward in purpose and power, let this truth remain in your heart forever: You will win. You are Powered for Success!

INDEX

PROPHETESS DR. MATTIE NOTTAGE, BA, MA, DD

Widely recognized as an accurate prophet to the nations, God used Prophetess Dr. Mattie Nottage to captivate audiences around the world with her prophetic, life-changing messages. Prophetess Nottage is married to Apostle Edison Nottage. She and her husband are the Founders and Senior Pastors of BFOMI GLOBAL Churches, which include churches in Georgia, Florida, Texas; Nassau, Bahamas; Pakistan; and more.

Mantled with an uncanny spirit of discernment and an undeniable, authentic, prophetic anointing for the ministry of deliverance, Prophetess Nottage is a well-respected international preacher, prolific teacher, motivational speaker, prayer coach, playwright, author, gospel recording artist, and revivalist. God uses this powerful yet humble woman of God extensively in the areas of the prophetic, deliverance, prayer, spiritual warfare, the supernatural, and the miraculous.

Whenever Prophetess Mattie Nottage prays and prophesies during her meetings, supernatural miracles, healing, and deliverance occur immediately in people's lives. Many phenomenal miracles, signs, and wonders follow her ministry.

She is the President and Founder of Mattie Nottage International Ministries, The Global Dominion Network Empowering Group of Companies, Women of Fire & Power Conference, The Youth A

Fire Transformation, Empowerment Mentoring Purpose program for Youth & Children, The Faith Village For Boys & Girls Transformation Program, and Chancellor of the prestigious Mattie Nottage Bible College. She is also the Founder of the one-of-a-kind Mattie Nottage Outstanding Kingdom Woman's Award.

Prophetess Nottage has ministered the gospel in places such as Ireland, Brazil, Africa, the Netherlands, throughout the United States of America, and the Caribbean. God uses her to "set the captive free" and to fan the flames of revival throughout the nations. Prophetess Nottage has an endearing passion for training and equipping individuals in spiritual warfare and prayer, enabling them to live a life of total victory.

She is the author of her bestselling books, including Encountering the God of Fire, 12 Minutes To Breakthrough Prayer Strategy, Why Everyone Needs Deliverance, and I Refuse To Die, along with numerous published works such as Breaking The Chains, From Worship to Warfare, I Still Want You-The Call To A Deeper Place, Prayer For The Annihilation and Assassination Of My Enemies, and many more.

She has also written a number of stage plays and songs, including the #1 smash-hit CD singles I Still Want You, Gonna Be A Great Night, Jesus Your Love Is All I Need, and In Jesus Name!

Prophetess Nottage hosts an online global prayer movement every weekday at 6:00 A.M. EST. She has appeared as a guest on various television networks, including The Trinity Broadcasting Network (TBN), The Word Network, Turning Point, One on One with Damon Davis, Atlanta Live TV, The Babbie Mason Talk Show "Babbie's House," and The Impact Network, among others.

Additionally, Prophetess Mattie Nottage has been featured in several magazines, including Preaching Woman and Gospel Today, as one of America's most influential pastors of her time. Prophetess Nottage is the former Chairman of the National Youth Advisory Council to the government of the Bahamas and was also recognized and awarded a "Proclamation of State" by the Mayor and Commissioner of Miami-Dade County, Florida, for her exemplary community initiatives that bring transformation and empowerment to the lives of youth and families globally.

Further, Prophetess Nottage has earned a Bachelor of Arts in Christian Counseling, a Master of Arts in Christian Education, and a Doctor of Divinity as a Prophet of Deliverance. She is widely known as God's Daughter of Fire and has fully committed her life to spreading the gospel of the Kingdom and to transforming the lives of people everywhere!

MINISTRY CONTACT INFORMATION

To request Dr. Mattie Nottage for a speaking engagement, an upcoming event, a life-coaching seminar, or a mentorship session, or to place an order for products, please contact:

Mattie Nottage Ministries, International
(U.S. Address)
MAILING ADDRESS:
3715 Bright Star Rd
Douglasville, GA 30135
1 (888) 825-7568
www.mattienottage.org

Follow us on:
Facebook @DrMattie Nottage
X @DrMattieNottage
YouTube @MattieNottageTV
Instagram @Drmattienottage
TikTok @drmattienottageofficial

Made in the USA
Monee, IL
12 September 2026

62976634R00090